NATURE IS ENOUGH

Essays for Freethinkers

Chris Highland

©2021 Chris Highland

Cover photo: Chris Highland

Friendly Freethinker

(www.chighland.com)

To
My Nieces and Nephews

"Every day I can see the sun as it gives me everything I need: heat, light, food, flowers in the park, reflections on the lake. An occasional skin cancer, but, hey! At least there are no crucifixions. And we sun worshippers don't go around killing other people simply because they don't agree with us.

Sun worship is fairly simple. There's no mystery, no miracles, no pageantry, no one asks for money, there are no songs to learn, and we don't have a special building where we all gather once a week to compare clothing. And the best thing about the sun. . .it never tells me I'm unworthy. It doesn't tell me I'm a bad person who needs to be saved. Hasn't said an unkind word. Treats me fine.

So I worship the sun. But I don't pray to the sun. You know why? Because I wouldn't presume on our friendship. It's not polite."

George Carlin

CONTENTS

INTRODUCTION

What sets this book apart from several earlier collections of essays is that these writings were not written as newspaper columns. *A Freethinker's Gospel*, *Broken Bridges* and *Friendly Freethinker* presented those columns to a wider audience. *Nature is Enough* offers a selection of essays from the last twenty years reflecting my life in the San Francisco Bay Area, then the Pacific Northwest and North Carolina. This book also has a clear and present theme: *Nature*. As simple as that sounds, Nature (which I often capitalize) covers pretty much anything and everything—not separate from humanity but radically all-encompassing. Each essay offers my curious thinking on the natural world, the extraordinary wonder, often exposed in the most ordinary.

I've written a good deal of my story elsewhere in books and blogs. Now, here, I'm opening up some rainsoaked, earthy and edgy essays that tell more of this landscape within—what I think about and feel in relation (or disconnect) with the human and non-human landscapes without. I've been spending more time turning the torn pages of my past, looking back on the pathways cut and chopped, dug and boot-raked, rather than being too concerned or distracted by the not-yet-found trails of an imagined land called "the future." Yet, I remain convinced of the underlying root, stream or ancient footpath behind and beneath these essays. I have a settled contentedness in knowing that whatever I find in the woods, meadows, rivers, mountains and wildlife—as well as in my mind's wild reaches—will provide a good, rich composting of lessons for me.

My wife Carol puts her heart into being a good teacher and counselor. I always tell her I couldn't do what she does (though I was a chaplain for decades and still teach). As she was describing the depth of conversations she was immersed in, a useful analogy came to mind; I said to her: "It's like you are wading into a person's life; if you kick around very much, you'll stir the mud, and that could muddy the water, and stick to you as well!" She liked that. Maybe the lesson is not so profound, but understanding ourselves, our inner world and human interactions, is intimately related to our experiences in the natural world. Of course that's true, naturally—we're a part of that world. We might say Nature is our "homeroom" teacher, and a damn good counselor, when we listen, when we're willing to wade in with her.

Nature is Enough wades in and stirs up some mud. That can be a good thing, or maybe not, but I try to hold the balance in my head: water can be clear and clean, *and* water can be a soup of sediment. Not bad versus good, but reality. That's one reason this book stirs up very few conclusions, and I guarantee you, no "divine" wisdom—only slick and muddy slipping along the edges of the riverbanks, the lakes, ocean cliffs, valleys and hollers where wild wondering ideas somehow flourish. I assure you, it'll be enough, for now.

Nature is "enough" of what? for what? for whom? The response will depend on each reader's perspective. I think these essays build on each other like waves of water, or sand, or wind or ideas. In the end I suspect my explorations will reveal a unified picture, a cohesive piece of art. Then again, maybe the reader will simply find the trail of thought bends into one perplexing question mark. If so, let it be.

Take heart, we have some competent guides along the trail ahead. John Muir's voice echoes throughout; his friends and fellow naturalists John Burroughs, Henry Thoreau and Teddy Roosevelt join the journey; Margaret Fuller drops some wisdom; Bertrand Russell, Frances Wright and Confucius call out to us; Walt Whitman and Mary Oliver walk along for a spell, so does Death, a dark mirror to give us a brighter glimpse into Life. The voices of Native Americans ring out and some unsheltered home-seekers can be heard as well —those landless human travelers we ignorantly call "homeless." And perhaps most importantly, I hope that the central voice in these pages is the chorus of wild things who lead us, if we leave our irrational fears behind, closer to wonder and our own wildness.

I'm handing you something of myself here. That

doesn't concern me, though it may help you keep in mind this is personal, even private in some ways. As we say these days, when we're honest—IMHO. These essays are my humble opinions. If there are lessons to be found, you'll need to find them, discover them for yourself. I can lead you to the tree, but I can't make you climb.

So I invite you to read, think, take a walk and think some more. Then, I'd be curious, as I am about everything in Nature, to know what you think.

Chris Highland
2021

1

Pathfinding

Opening the Classroom

I suppose it's true that from time to time it helps to look back down the trail to get a better sense of where we've been, and maybe where we're going. About ten years back, during a short sabbatical in my native Northwest, I lived in a tiny, one-room cabin at a retreat center. When I wasn't writing or exploring nearby parks and shorelines I was helping around the land chopping and stacking wood, mowing, weeding, gardening, fence-repairing and the like. The director asked if I would create a pathway from the parking area to the main building—probably seventy-five yards. I stumbled and crawled through the thick undergrowth beneath cedar, maple, fir and elderberry looking for some important clues.

First, I tried to be aware of the natural contours and openings where the forest "moves" with the earth. Second, I looked for existing natural trails made by those who live in the forest, on the land, in the earth: the deer, raccoons, foxes, rabbits as well as the smaller squirrels, mice, shrews, even slugs, beetles and spiders. Third, I noticed where a trail might hold secure in heavy rains and heavy foot traffic. Fourth, I got down close to see where roots and root systems protruded from the ground so as to avoid harming these major arteries for the life of the trees. Then, as I began to clip, cut and clear what I determined to be "the best way," I kept in constant mindfulness that I was causing harm to a wild area while at the same time opening up the area for human participation through movement and hopefully mindfulness, respect, appreciation.

A few autumns later I was working on a forty-five acre farm that is largely forest rich in alder, cedar, fir, hemlock, maple, blackberry vines, huckleberry and blueberry bushes, elderberry "trees" and much more. There are marshes, bogs and small wetland drains. There are dark, hidden groves and bright, sun-lit open spaces. Here I grew further into my own style of mindful pathclearing, creating a trail system that meanders, loops, backtracks and crisscrosses the land through all kinds of terrain. The work gave a tree-mendous amount of satisfaction to me (the ghost of dad's puns, sorry). The physical exertion—stretching, lifting, sawing, swinging of machete, sweat, scratches, aches, blood and all—was immensely exhilarating, though at times frustrating. The time alone with Nature's instruction was, to put it mildly, inspiring.

From my work I have begun to draw some preliminary lessons about life that may or may not apply to another person, yet I feel compelled to pass along a few leafy branches, sticks or seeds from the wild classroom.

Entering the Gates of Wildness

When I first walked on the farm and deep into the forest on old lumber roads now grassy, mossy and green, it was obvious that people had not only been out there before but had been there with a purpose: *production*. The felling of trees was the industry and they utilized horses, trucks and even a small train to haul out the logs. Large old stumps appear sometimes when looking a little closer at a thicket of rich moss, ferns and huckleberries. The stump monuments cause one to reflect on the activities of the past yet are a constant reminder of the resilience and creativity of Nature in the present and for the future—how the natural sculpting of the "deadness" is forever being shaped into a fecund "newness of life."

So I entered through the thick tangle of brush and bush to seek paths, trails to circle out into the far reaches of the land. Here I gripped another rule of (green) thumb that I add to the principles of path-clearing listed above. The landowners and I pointed to stands of trees or one large tree (particularly a grove or individual cedar) a half-acre or so off, and said, "Haven't seen that up close. Be nice to find a way to walk there." This sense of intriguing curiosity drew me to head in the direction of identified trees. Guided by an orienteering, a positioning related to a towering cedar, maple or hemlock, kept me "on track" and gave a reference point for the movement forward. Then, taking into account the other principles learned earlier, I could move along to wind toward the "marker" ahead.

There is nothing "straight forward" about this work. One landowner was delighted that the trails I cleared were not simply functional point-A-to-point-B kinds of lines. Of course I have a bias toward sauntering, and the land itself almost invites a kind of snaking, twisting, more "organic" walking. I keep in mind Thoreau's musing in his essay "Walking": "I have met with but one or two persons in the course of my life who understood the art of Walking, that is, of taking walks—who had a genius, so to speak, for sauntering." At times I am drawn to turn a trail nearly back upon itself which not only makes possible the viewing of where you have just been, but offers a backward glance at what you would miss had you not turned, and turned there at that spot.

It seems appropriate at this point on the path to mention Thoreau's warning: "I am alarmed when it happens that I have walked a mile into the woods bodily, without getting there in spirit." Personally, I would find much less satisfaction in clearing a trail merely for the functionality (bodily use) of it than for the educational, even inspirational ("spiritual") opportunity the opening provides. I know only too well what Thoreau was feeling when alarmed at his own neglecting or forgetting of the beauty and lessons into which he had sauntered. For the most remarkable aspect of pathclearing, as for sauntering itself, is that one is truly opening a sylvan gate into a never-before-seen classroom or sanctuary. This baptism is full immersion. The good, mindful pathfinder/clearer works to open trails for the passing of feet without ever forgetting the open minds, thoughts, eyes, visions, hearts and souls that will also pass there, and perhaps pause there.

Tangles Without, Tangles Within

Theodore Roosevelt, after his humiliating defeat for re-election in 1912, set off on another of his famous adventures that had earlier included African safaris. This was to be a dangerous, even life-threatening expedition into a mysterious part of the Amazon basin, to travel along a legendary tributary of the great river. This journey was to last six grueling months (October 1913-April 1914) and drive the ex-president to the edge of suicide. After weeks of frustrating travels just to get positioned for the push northward, the huge party of men, mules and oxen were faced with crossing the Brazilian highlands. At one point they had to hack their way through a dense tropical jungle. Roosevelt wrote, "Away from the broad, beaten route every step of a man's progress represented slashing a trail with the machete through the tangle of bushes, low trees, thorny scrub, and interlaced creepers" (Candace Millard, *River of Doubt*, 2005). The bully, progressive president was tough, yet, bullied by the wild, this kind of "progress" almost defeated him for a second, more serious, more permanent time.

I know a little of that feeling of fatigue and defeat. On a much smaller scale though (I learned from Millard that Brazil is 250,000 square miles larger and the Amazon longer than the contiguous United States). More than once I have faced down some thorny obstacles that nearly defeated my progress, where every yard forward took exertion equal to twenty feet in less thorny thickets. One area I called "blackberry hell" took me several days to have my literal breakthrough. Some of the berry stalks were as thick as small trees. The thorns scratched my hands, legs, face and tore my clothing, often sticking me through my leather gloves, and made me curse when a vine reached over and picked the hat off my head (that indignity seemed almost intentional!).

Thorns and thickets, dense woodlands, can teach many lessons. Their wisdom becomes clear when one attempts to forge a path where either it really is impossible to transverse a pathway, or the challenge is too much for the energy level (or the mental capacity) of the pathclearer. While working on a particularly tangled section of a four-acre parcel I found myself stuck, in more ways than one. I thought I knew the best way to cut through to a fallen cedar that looked inviting from ten yards away. I tried two hack jobs that were indeed hack jobs. I felt sorry and told the trees so. I also felt defeated and stupid. I had to back out and seek out another practical way. Sure, if I had a handy chainsaw (or dynamite) I could have made a wide thoroughfare. But I called myself the Mindful Machete Man for a reason! I can't do such destructive harm, though I may have felt like blasting on a few times. I merely cursed my idiocy and backed out of the density to lick my wounds, whine to the forest and take a walk to cool off.

In the "Great Rite" ceremony of the Wiccan tradition there is a line that says, "Open for me the secret way, The pathway of intelligence, Beyond the gates of night and day, Beyond the bounds of time and sense. Behold the mystery aright–."   Bold and noble words. There are secret ways to be found. Not all could be opened or ought to be. When I am out there, alone with the forest and its creatures, I often feel beyond the bounds of time and sense, and up to my chin in mystery. A powerful, humbling realization it is. Maybe I am not a stranger or an invader of the forestland, yet it is not where I live, at least at present. I do sense a particular and peculiar relation with these wild spots and am continually, often painfully, aware of my intrusion. But the reality remains. Like John Muir, I go out in order to go in—inward, to a wild place, an unexplored space, within. I know a little of Muir's exuberance and enthusiasm for the wilderness, even the wild nearby in a rural forest or garden. I also have a feeling for Roosevelt's attraction, perhaps addiction, to exploration and discovery. If we have listened closely to modern biologists, we might actually see ourselves, each and all, as explorers and potential discoverers, since we are told that most species on earth have neither been cataloged or even discovered. As one who senses a certain urge to clear paths, to see what I, and others, may never have seen otherwise, I am thrown back on the wonder of what is beneath my bootsoles; what is being sliced through with each blow of the machete; and what mysteries might be cut open before me as I "make my way" into regions that are never, ultimately, mine at all.

Bounding across Boundaries

I cut, chopped, sawed and cracked a path to the boundary marker, the Northeast corner of the land marked by a cement slab, a metal pole and numerous bright-pink streamers. Clearing the area to make it more visible, I stopped to wipe the sweat, to pull a leaf off my neck, and to consider boundaries. This exposes a critical issue and concern I often faced in non-profit work. Alongside colleagues and staff, we were always concerned with questions of boundaries. Where does my work cross over into personal areas better left untouched? Are there gray areas? Who sets the boundary lines and why? Could there not be times, situations and circumstances when the boundaries could be "violated" for greater good and purposes? Many of the questions remained unclear with no absolutes. I still feel that way, particularly relating to relationships with land, the earth, Nature itself. When I was a chaplain, people sometimes challenged my decisions regarding boundaries. For instance, one day I would deny access to our office to someone who was obviously drunk. The next day I would allow another person who had been drinking to enter, to sit, to join in a group session. When I didn't simply cop out and answer the complainer with "Well, it's My decision," I would try to explain the rationale for the "inconsistency." It might be based on my knowledge of the individuals involved and their level of "management" of their addictions. For example, I knew that one guy drank a lot but he was fairly respectful of our work and would rarely disrupt. Another guy was notorious for disrupting everything and disrespecting everyone. In split second decisions, I or other staff might choose to allow one and deny another, even if no words were spoken. We simply had a history and "saw it coming."

In relation to the land and pathclearing there are similar principles at work. Primarily, naturally, the earth has no boundaries but those we impose artificially. I have a software program that shows the earth as seen from space. I can click on a "boundaries" button in the tool bar and the globe is instantly divided up in lines and nation-states. Another button will simply show the topography of the land. Yet another will show colors not appearing in satellite imagery. The point may be clear: We choose how to view the earth and what divides the earth. Personal property issues aside, Nature has only the mountains, the rivers, dense forests, deserts, masses of ice, oceans and such that perhaps separate species one from another. I want my space and piece of the earth as much as anyone, yet I am also conscious of the fact that I could never personally own this piece of Nature, that bit of dirt, and what grows and lives in that dirt. Human arrogance has blinded us from this reality but Nature and her processes regularly remind us of the futility of our rights to absolute ownership and control. An earthquake shifts the boundaries of land; a tsunami washes away property; a hurricane or tornado obliterates fences, signposts and whole neighborhoods. What can we depend on? Not much, if we seek permanent stability, solid boundaries.

We have a history. We "see it coming." We know how we act and how Nature acts. My pathclearing work took months on many acres of land. I mapped out the trail system and could hand it to others to walk the land. Yet, to be truthful, Winter was often at the door with his winds, rains and snows, and everyone knows that Spring will come and she will take back that which is "cleared." For these paths to remain "open" they will need to be "maintained," continually cleared. Not long after clearing a trail I found fallen branches and whole trees that blocked the paths I once opened. Like green doorways, trails open, and trails close. It is a truism: Nature takes back what belongs to it. Another truism is that Nature incessantly does its own opening, and closing. That's true for a trail, and it's true for the humans who saunter trails of our own clearing. We too will be cleared away (by the Greater Pathclearer, Nature) to keep open the way of Life on Earth. One closes, another clears, opens. This keeps it all in perspective doesn't it? And I cannot allow myself to be tricked into thinking my paths, my boundaries, my way will even exist in a short time to come (I take some comfort imagining what I cleared has now been reclaimed, even by the blackberries) A good reminder. An essential twisting, tangle of wisdom. Perhaps the greatest lesson. And one I have learned as an opener, a finder, a pathclearer in the Nature I love and respect.

What new ground is yet to open before me, before you, before us? What secret rooms, closets, attics and basements of our World-home have never been seen by human eyes? And, maybe not all should be seen. I'm content with that. But I can't let go of the curiosity of a pathfinder, knowing the ultimate accomplishment is not the trail cut clear and complete. It is the moment when the gloves come off, the sweat is wiped by the tattered cub-scout kerchief (carried for 50 years), the saw is laid down, the machete is leaned against a tree, the mattock is set on a log, and I lay back on a curving cedar trunk, looking up into the tangle of scented branches, and sense, deep in my own roots, that I am not the only pathfinder or pathmaker active in this forest; I am one of countless workers seeking my way, laboring and resting here.

2010

2

Dirty Glaciers

"Doubling cape after cape, passing uncounted
islands, new combinations break on the view
in endless variety, sufficient to satisfy the lover
of wild beauty through a whole life."
~John Muir, Travels in Alaska

On a family journey one summer we ventured by car, plane, bus, train, ship and boots into the still-wild lands of Alaska. We saw the rugged and majestic peak of Denali (McKinley if you prefer), observed grizzlies and caribou, mountain sheep and fox, moose and eagles. Coming back down the Inside Passage on the Marine Highway the jagged mountains, ice-cold whale-blessed waters and emerald islands gathered around us with a deep, dark sense of wonder and mystery. There is nothing like the wilderness for restoring the feeling of relation, connection (perhaps more meaningful words than "spiritual"). Honestly, at times it seems too big—-a frightening kinship with distant relatives I'm not sure I really want to know too intimately!

One can be grateful that a little over 100 years ago

Theodore Roosevelt had the vision to preserve over 20 million acres of forested land in Southeastern Alaska (Tongass, Chugach and the Alexander Archipelago). TR's expansive instincts, so infuriating to some, set aside something grander, something even our wildest imagination cannot get a hold of. And so it must be.

As we enjoyed the rather leisurely, buoyant experience, I read some of my favorite passages from John Muir in his memoir, Travels in Alaska. Since I consider Muir one of Nature's chaplains I once again delighted in his delight and recalled my decision a few years back to transform super-natural faith into natural delight.

Up in the northland where there is still a palpable feeling of frontier, we learned more of First Nations culture while visiting museums, reading historical pieces and speaking with Native Alaskans (we stopped for lunch in Wasilla, but the only ex-governor sightings were on calendars and coloring books). The raw emotion of the injustice done to the aboriginal people by our culture and religion was painfully present. I felt taken back over one hundred years to the time when Muir was exploring this same land. Stepping off his ship into an old Stickeen village south of Wrangell, Muir thought it strange that the missionaries were so interested in a deserted place. Before he witnessed the chopping down of the sacred totem poles by the party, he exulted in pure Muirian language:

"Divinity abounded nevertheless; the day was divine and

there was plenty of natural religion in the newborn land-scapes that were being baptized in sunshine, and sermons in the glacial boulders on the beach where we landed."

The Scotsman of Yosemite, forced to memorize scriptures as a child, utilized the old language to express a wider, more inclusive spirituality undistracted by super-naturalism. Unafraid of immersion in the wild beauty, he was fully disgusted by the actions of those who came to that land to alter it with altars, to tame its wilderness and wild people who called it home. Thankfully it appears they were not completely successful (sure is satisfying at times to see how profoundly some ancestors failed in their efforts to impose their will and their way, isn't it?

Our ship sailed deep into Glacier Bay. Like some living cathedral (only better), it was akin to sailing straight into a sanctuary where the roofless beauty leaves you speechless. We drew near to the Margerie Glacier with its 350-foot wall of crystal-blue ice. Unlike anything I'd ever seen, the dramatic "calving" of huge chunks of ice made for quite a silencing show. In close proximity to the Margerie is the Grand Pacific Glacier that stretches across the border from Canada. This glacier is the widest in the bay (2 miles). With frigid water below, frosty air all around, and ice shelves as far as your eye can see, you almost feel you're inside the refrigerator/freezer of the world.

This naturalist lesson only highlights an observation. On our visit the entire ship was focused, with eager expectation, on the cracking and crumbling drama of the Margerie. This was completely understandable since the Grand Pacific, even though 25 miles long and the widest, is covered in dark rock and dirt. It is what is referred to as a "dirty glacier." It doesn't draw attention and just isn't as full of sexy drama as its more spectacular neighbor. Few cameras were focused on the muddy mammoth.

I suppose it's time to draw the connections, to make my point about "spiritual things" and ethics. For a number of years I served as an interfaith chaplain, first with mentally exceptional adults, then in a county jail and finally on the streets with "residentially challenged" people. I ventured into many dark, damp and dirty places to practice a presence of compassion. To sum up the experiences I might simply describe the scene I witnessed: Commanding the center of attention was business and busyness, money and work, traffic, and the frantic and frenzied scramble to get more. In this madness stood the faith community, theology and study of sacred books, ritual, tradition and great talk about something called "community." Many stood or sat mesmerized by the drama, expectantly awaiting the next chunk of exhilarating wisdom to come sliding down from the pulpit of pastor or professor. Off to the side, rather hidden (though in full view if one cared to notice), was the very un-dramatic and ever disturbing, uncomfortable and offensive distraction of the unclean, the dirty ones.

What emerged from all this mucking around in the muck was a Copernican revolution in my thinking and vocation. My Glacier Bay moment came like a cold arctic wind. What are we seeing? What are we not seeing? It makes all the difference. Seriously. We cannot practice any form of ethics without a fresh formation of seeing, of sight, of vision.

The troubling term "wild" is disturbing for a reason. This is not a place where we immediately feel a belonging, though the expansive beauty attracts and seduces our senses. But somehow we know that we indeed do belong, it is a part of us and we of it. As Robert Macfarlane puts it: "I had learned to see another type of wildness, to which I had once been blind: the wildness of natural life, the sheer force of ongoing organic existence, vigorous and chaotic" (*The Wild Places*). The land is us, not merely this state or that nation, not a clickable map or political coloring book. In seeing the wild we see if not sense our own wildness and the essential need to care for that somehow, some way.

A tour-guide on the train directed our attention to the vast green open spaces and said something I thought was a joke, but I don't think it was: "Just keep looking out there and you'll see things that don't seem to fit—those are the animals." I just shook my head in amazement at that level of ignorance. Who doesn't fit out there? Who would perish in a very short time in this country? A local bus driver boasted that he gets an annual oil dividend check along with all Alaskans, using part of it to hunt caribou, moose and bear, and of course catch just about all the salmon he wants. He was so proud. We were so shocked. With short-sightedness the open spaces of wild beauty become what one lumber company executive called "resource inventory systems."

An environmental ethics is needed that includes all ethical systems because the environment is our teacher, text and tradition. In other words, there can be no ethics or "spiritual practice" without an immersion in the great classroom and sanctuary that is Nature. Muir knew it, felt it, lived it. So did his friends John Burroughs and Teddy Roosevelt. We need to listen, and get dirty; we need "dirty" ethics.

In one of the most stunning passages in his journals, John of the Mountains wrote, *"No synonym for God is so perfect as Beauty. Whether as seen carving the lines of the mountains with glaciers, or gathering matter into stars. . .still all is Beauty!"* (June 26, 1875). Did Muir see the dirt? Clearly he did. Was he sensitive to the turmoil and tragedy, the disease, death and destruction on the planet? No doubt. Yet for wonder-filled ("spiritual") explorers like Muir there is no separation from the dirty glaciers of our existence, no disconnection from the wild beauty of our surrounding, embracing home, except in our minds.

To the extent our religious traditions acknowledge

and celebrate the connections, they have relevance. To the extent our "spirituality" can see and value and participate in the hidden wonders, it has meaning. If we can call any God we choose "Beauty" then maybe, just maybe, we can accept the dirt as beautiful and practice an ethic that encompasses all points of the compass, as people of the land, the ground, the dirt, the water, the grinding glaciers still carving our heavenly, better-than-any-heaven-you-can-make-up, home.

2011

3

Eulogy for a Pond

A portion of this essay was published in the South Whidbey Record

Henry David Thoreau famously wrote about the big puddle he built his shack alongside, where he chose to make a livelihood for two years in 1840s Massachusetts. He scrambled the edges and from his scrambles came scribbled notes, dribbled on damp pages.

"Formerly I had come to this pond adventurously, from time to time. . .But now I had made my home by the shore." (*Walden*)

I know something of pondside, bayside, riverside, oceanside, Sound-side living. I was born and soaked in the salt and the sod of rich, saturated Pacific Northwest soil. I'm no Thoreau, and where I lived was no Walden, though in some way, in my mind at least, it was a mirror of that other coast, another cabin-on-lake. The puddle that concerned me was visible from my cabin window, squatting its muddy bottom as I did on this forty-mile island in the Puget Sound (Salish Sea). I wrote this eulogy for another tree-shaded circle of water; another lakelet leaking life day by day.

"A lake is the landscape's most beautiful and expressive feature. It is earth's eye; looking into which the beholder measures the depth of [their] own nature."

I might call this Peat Pond, and I sometimes do, if it needs a name, and it doesn't. This small acre of wet, fed by natural artesian springs, the runoff of seasonal streams"—burns" the Scots would say—is drained to be of use as a peat bog each summer. The pond becomes a ditch. It is scraped and dug for saleable soil—at least the decompositions of what life once composed here. A raft with a pump floats on the dark water, a pipe stretches to shore, jetting a spray of minute creatures in the wash high in the air. Leaky irrigation, or do the horses drink its draught? I watch each evening as the water level falls. On my sunset saunters along the shore I step quietly and alert in the green grasses. In winter months I took photographs of the frozen brown blades, the play of light and shadows on the layers of ice and snow, slanting sun reaching far out onto the frozen water beyond, where I dare not step.

This spring attracted a steady stream of Canada geese who trespass as I do. They wake me each morning with first light and call me to appreciate the sinking sun each evening. A few weeks ago I stood still as a cedar to observe two proud geese gliding like feathered bookends off shore with six tiny goslings hurrying along between. Several nights later, three ducklings trailed their parents around the shoreline circumference.

A great blue heron (not as blue as it is great) comes and goes like a dignitary—an ambassador from a near and borderless country gliding in for the banquet.

In a late day's warm winds, a white-crested eagle circles off the glistening waters. Passing low over my bare and balding head it banks near enough to these banks to hear a bit of music in the feathers.

A few more cautious, alert steps and my eye is drawn upward to a large sharp-shinned hawk caught in its own skyward whirlpool, only slightly distracted by pursuing swallows, persistent, encircling.

At nightfall, the call of coyotes pierces the dark with their wild yelps. The rabbits munching, jumping and humping all around my cabin set back in the woods become a munching themselves when the light dissolves. Pairs of Barred Owls, never barred from their nocturnal hunts, enter the feasting, while rabbits, squirrels, mice, treefrogs and other invisibles climb on the plate to participate in the feast.

The cabin-dweller of Concord, who opened, as I do, his one-room to the room of the woods, guessed his pond may well have been named for the stony hills surrounding it—thus it became, Walled-in Pond.

I set foot here, disembarked on this isle, to shake off the walls and have fewer of them, to write, to grow a fresh livelihood, to settle a more simplified life. As the

Walden wanderer I too wished to make myself "neighbor to the birds." I wonder now if the winged ones are neighbors in need—their life, like mine, threatened with an incessant squeezing, a slow pumping away and selling off of our wild neighborhood.

As I watch the trees fall, cringe at the crack and thump of their wasted weight; as I hear the all-too-familiar whine of the saws and rumble of the dozers that never sleep; and as I watch twilight by twilight the pond fall, walled-in more and more by people building and dogs barking—I cannot help this eulogy for the land, its eye, the reflective sky, and ask: as my island of peace drains and disappears into marketable peat and timber, ringed by rusted machinery—what of the goslings, ducklings, ascending eagles, herons and hawks? What of the frogs who sing their Beethoven's Ninth each night, and of the unseen homesteads beneath my feet? What of their island, my island, our island? What of the earth?

I wish to say a blessing, a "rest in peace."
If I find words to say I find I must say these words,
"I'm sorry. There is no rest. This is no peace."
We are forever walled-in.

I walk away, deeper into a shallower wood, silently turning back but once.
A season is passing. And so is a pond.

2007

4

I Sing the Body Electricity

*"I am drawn by its breath as if I were no more
than a helpless vapor, all falls aside but myself
and it, Books, art, religion, time, the visible and
solid earth, and what was expected of heaven
or fear'd of hell, are now consumed. . . ."*
~Walt Whitman, "I Sing the Body Electric"

I was awakened in the middle of the night, not by thunder but eerily quiet electric sky. Dark shapeless clouds spread over the eastern hills like a mass of algae on an inverted sea. Standing naked at the shadeless window to watch the intermittent explosions across the fields over the bay, I thought of the air on fire, of the earth too, even the ocean, and of the catastrophic conflagration of flight 447 suddenly lost over the Atlantic out of Rio. *Kata-strophe*: "to turn down; the final event of the dramatic action, especially of a tragedy." High drama brought low. The turn down, into death, into a conflagration—a burning fire of destruction. The beauty of the fire in the sky that night seared the silence of death over the sea into my vision. It was tragically beautiful.

John Muir saw the fires in the sky, and in the forest, and mountains and rivers. Like all good naturalists, he had an eye for the fire within all things—the Heraclitian life that animates the world. He once wrote (in *Our National Parks*) of a mighty earthquake in Yosemite Valley, describing it as Mother Nature bouncing us upon her knee. The force of Nature was not something to be feared but learned from, even delighted in—we're kin after all. In saying that "all Nature's wildness tells the same story" he exults in the music of that wild tale, shaken to the bone with the crazy wisdom of storms, that whether they be "torrents, earthquakes, cataclysms, 'convulsions of nature', etc., however mysterious and lawless at first sight they may seem, are only harmonious notes in the song of creation. . . ." In that trembling night Muir was not endangered and no lives were lost. Yet, maybe he was identifying a profound fact often forgotten in the way we cope with "natural" calamities (*calamitas*: "destruction; state of deep distress") and cataclysms (*cataclysmos:* "a violent washing"). We are not in control (an oft-forgotten truth), and certainly not masters of anything except perhaps our own reactions—our responses to what occurs naturally—sometimes mysteriously, but always naturally.

A nephew of mine wrote to raise some contemporary issues with the ancient ideas of Plato in *The Republic*. The time-honored questions of idealism and the supernatural, distilled down, in my young relative's mind, to the sobering understanding that we can't control the beyond, the supra-physical, only the earth-bound, tangible and temporary. One can only be honest to speak about the known and the knowable, not guess at the unknown and perhaps unknowable. We are too quick to turn our guesses into knowledge or fact. Were Plato and Socrates plugging in to the main current of wisdom when they considered the soul some kind of booted up body and vice versa?

In Walt Whitman's famous poem he sings of his own body's electricity. It was in a day when electrical power was only beginning to be fully understood and "harnessed" (an anthropomorphic fiction tricking ourselves that the environment can be domesticated). Whitman celebrated the lightning in his own protoplasm, in his flesh, his bones and brain. He was charged with life and the living of it, fully juiced, amped up as we might say today. His "song" is amplified early in the great section of *Leaves of Grass* (his incarnational book that hit America with its own shocking bolt), the section Whitman named "Children of Adam." Born of the earthly, virescent Eden, garden-dweller, the Poet of the Cosmos (so honored by John Burroughs) is compelled to march with "the armies of those I love" whom he charges "full with the charge of the soul."

If you are familiar with the electrified poet you are aware that Walt's soul is "not more than the body" ("Song of Myself") and here he asks with full volume of extended lungs, "if the body were not the soul, what is the soul?" Whitmans' electricity is not only palpable here but catastrophic—a dramatic turn down to the earth. If we think he is simply and narcissistically "getting himself off" in these thundering passages of sex, procreation, and creative tension, that this is only another tune repeated from "Song of Myself," we are ill-prepared to head into the storm with him—we hit the towering, ion-packed thunderheads over the ocean as he drives us in, face to face with the high, punishing winds of the slave auction.

He steps in to "sell" a man, then a woman, on the auction block—both naked, representative people (as Emerson might say, and did), both dark human beings standing upon the dark pedestal of inhumanity yet illumined as a lightning storm for who they are—they stand, literally, for us, for America, for humanity.

Whitman "sells" these human slaves, liberated by the cataclysm of their sheer humanness, and in his electric ecstasy he concludes his composition, this horrible exhibition without inhibition in the public square, with the "likes" of the parts of the human body zapped with power, piece by throbbing (whipped and scarred) piece. He is a child of Adam, of Eve, of the Mother and Father of the planet, of God, of Slavery, of Revolution, of the Poet writ large in neon lights upon the clouds, because every part of him is lit up by being wired to everything. For Whitman, seller of slaves, was selling himself, his own body, with every sale. He lists, graphically, comprehensively, all the parts of the body (read "soul" or "poem" or "human existence"), parts long hidden, shameful and sacred, singing self-consciously:

"The curious sympathy one feels when feeling with the hand the naked meat of the body, the circling rivers the breath ... the thin red jellies within you or within me. O I say these are not the parts and poems of the body only, but of the soul, O I say now these are the soul!"

Only the soloist on his auction-block stage, singing such an earthly and ground-bound pile of leaves collected into his grassy opus could draw us all into a soulful chorus that identifies the soul with the body, the "spiritual" melting into the material, fully conscious of the beauty, the injustice, the clear skies of day and the dark, dangerous, atmospheric illuminations of the sparking sky. This song on the breeze brings a note of dread and discovery; a calamity in the clouds above and within. A new truth is strangely attractive in its dissonance. The "soul" may be simply, scientifically and spiritually, the electrified body, synapses and syncopation in the song of flesh, bone and thin red jellies.

The "souls" who perished in the night sky high over the Atlantic, like perhaps those slaves sold by a rapturous poet, may have, in their final moments, witnessed the catastrophe, the final tragic event, of the drama of supercharged Nature, when body and soul unite in life's crescendo. In that moment, is it all clear in the bright darkness of life's unbounded energy? When Death and Life meet in an instant as do Body and Soul, are they seen for what they are, felt, experienced in a flash as undivided, inseparable, identical?

Undeserving of such an ending, perhaps those who have rained upon our ocean planet, in some shocking sense, were worthy, privileged of a death—a turning down of life—in the awesome brightness of the explosive, electric sky.

2008

5

The Phone Tree

I called her after nine in the evening that first night in the tiny one-room, cedar-shingled cabin with the bamboo ladder reaching to the cozy loft overhead. Another dramatic relocation for the nomadic gypsy in me. When I returned to my homestate to briefly settle in the basement of an island home overlooking the bay and mountains I kept my dream of living in a cabin in the woods. Now it was a reality. Smaller than anywhere I had ever lived, its isolation and rustic nature were balanced by the new power-line (one outlet), compost toilet and well-water just a short walk away down a winding tree- and berry-lined path.

I knew my wireless phone would let me say hello at best. I had checked the reception earlier and it was not good—only one bar on the screen. I called my close friend Heather from my forest hideaway and though she lives in Oregon and I was resettling in Washington I did not want to be on an island of isolation. I looked forward to a shared excitement and words of encouragement. She had seen me through nine moves over the years and knew exactly how it felt to finally find just the right spot to make a home.

Heather's phone rang and I waited, knowing she was there but unsure whether she would make it to the phone in time. Her house in the Rogue River valley is a mansion compared to my cabin and she could be out in her spacious gardens watering or taking a late evening walk with a glass of wine. I began leaving a message and she picked up. "I'm here. I'm here!" she panted. "We were just finishing dinner and I wasn't sure I could get to the phone in time. How are you? Are you in the cabin? How does it feel?" Being a great cook and baker she knew how to pepper me with questions.

As I began to tell her about the day she interrupted. "You're cutting out. I can barely hear you." I tried again and it was clear that my voice was anything but clear. I stood and went out onto the deck beneath the stars and silhouetted trees surrounding in all directions. "I can hear you a little better now" she said. "Yes, I can hear you very nicely" I replied. I went on with the story of my day of cleaning the old place and arranging my meager possessions in a new place. Then she laughed. "You sound like a strobe. You're cutting out and then coming back." So I started to repeat sentences, then phrases, then words. Heather laughed more and I joined her. For the next half hour or so I spoke in repetitive phrases and words ("I love it here--I love it here;" "The stars and moon are beautiful—are beautiful"). Even Heather started repeating words and we could not stop laughing. Finally we agreed that speaking this way was getting old very fast. I told her, "I'm gonna try to find a 'phone tree' and call you later in the week." I guess she heard that because she said she would think of me and talk with me soon. Shutting the flip-phone was a relief … a relief.

The next day I continued to settle into my new cabin, cleaning and organizing the storage boxes trying to make every square foot count. On my list for the day, just below "clean the windows" and "bring dad's lilac in the gator [tractor]," was "phone tree."

I slipped into my walking shoes, threw on a hat and grabbed my little folding phone, tucking it into my shirt pocket. I set out down a forest path I had cleared in past months heading for a tree I had paused beside and pondered by the pond (well really it was a marsh, so I suppose I mused). I remembered wiping the sweat with my old, ragged cub-scout kerchief and looking up: "You would be a good climbing tree. I'm coming back to climb you." In a few minutes of hurtling roots and pushing aside bright green, sprouting salmonberry branches I stood under the cedar. Behind a sturdy evergreen huckleberry bush I found a low, living limb for the first step up. It was an easy climb but I took some time, clearing away short dead sticks. Half way up I checked my phone: still only one bar—poor reception. I continued upward, getting the scented sap on my hands and strands of lichen in my hair.

Resting on a perfect perch near the top I looked down without seeing the ground. All I could observe from high up there was green life—trees in all directions. Not a house or a person; not a road or a light. Carefully drawing my phone from my shirt pocket I was mindful that it would be a long drop if the cell slipped from my hand. I lifted its gray metallic lid and the light illuminated the connection: *three bars*. I had good reception.

The call went through and I heard my sister's voice loud and clear. "I'm calling from my phone tree," I said while she giggled with laughter. Describing the lofty sight and the balance and sway to her, she thought it was crazy but appropriate for me. She knew I loved climbing trees. This was a natural for me. A few minutes later I called Heather. Delighted by the call and the location I was calling from she wanted to know all the details about my move and the cabin, what she couldn't pick up in the echoes of the other night. As we spoke, a light rain began to fall and I leaned closer against the gently rotating trunk. Concerned I might get electrocuted or fall Heather encouraged me to descend but I was in my element. "No, this is great. The tree is protecting me from the rain and I feel secure on these limbs," I assured her.

When we hung up I was still hanging up there, in the natural antenna-tower of the cedar. I breathed deeply and wiped wetness from my eyes—a mingling of tears and rain. I knew I could stay in touch, that I could enjoy my solitude without being isolated, that I could be reached and could make calls by reaching up and up, climbing the heights of this original, more natural, living telephone pole. The lines were open; I was receptive. As a robin, a jay and a chickadee went about their flighty business below me—below me!—, a Great Horned Owl called out from a marshy grove a little way off. I smiled, nodding, bobbing on the branch with emotion—I had never felt higher after a cellphone conversation. I had some roots in the forest and now a place in the leafy boughs to sit as I would, in the island woods, in my private phone tree.

2006

6

Lessons from the Treetops

"A new manifestation is at hand, a new hour is come. We would have every arbitrary barrier thrown down. We would have every path laid open to Woman as freely as to Man. Were this done, we believe a divine energy would pervade nature to a degree unknown in the history of former ages."
~Margaret Fuller, Woman in the Nineteenth Century

This Sunday morning talk was given at the Unitarian-Universalist Congregation of Whidbey Island, meeting under the trees on their land, before the new "sanctuary" was built

I grew up in a tradition with many branches, rooted in scriptures and creeds written on libraries full of pages chopped and carved from living trees. It was as if the original leaves or bark were torn from their environment and erased of all their original messages, then etched over with artificial doctrines.

This, my first public talk on Whidbey Island, reflects my new roots, my renewed sense of listening for the teachings offered by the free university of the wild, the living sources of the natural world written for all to see.

These are now my essential texts. Forests of libraries are now open to me. It is here, near to the earth, where I delightfully find a spiritual path that now and again leads straight up a tree.

Have you ever been to heaven? I found my way there the other day. I walked out to Partridge Point along the bluffs. As John Muir would say, it was *glorious*. Blue skies, warm sun glistening off the Sound, birds singing and autumn colors painting their art show finest. As I was sauntering along the bluff I said to myself—it was almost a prayer—, "What am I seeing? What am I not seeing?" A few moments later, for some reason, I glanced back up to see some picnickers looking intently out to the waters. I looked to see what they might be spying. A puff of spray rose about a half-mile off shore. Then others. I've seen many blows from gray whales but then I saw the high, black fins: Orca! Five, then seven surfaced. Then others, until I would guess I saw fifteen or more. A moment of heaven. I was grateful and thanked *Good Nature* for the gift of these incredible creatures of our common waterways.

A great lesson. What do we see? What do we not see? And the second is like unto the first: What am I *hearing*? What am I not hearing? This lesson slapped me into full consciousness when I put my head to the side and realized I could hear the blow of the spray from the pod at they moved up the Strait! A remarkable, heavenly moment.

I found another way into heaven when I was a boy growing up in Lake Forest Park and then Edmonds. I had a kind of secret love. It wasn't whales at that point. It was a love of climbing trees. There was a strong boyish thrill in climbing the ladder of branches up to my own perch nested in the upper branches. From there I could scan over the neighborhood, spying a little on the people next door, and not be seen by anyone. It was my secret place. Only the curious birds and squirrels knew of my presence. If my parents had known that I was so high up they might have called me down and scolded. Or maybe not. They knew I loved being outside and would rather be outdoors than indoors, in any season.

Since those younger days I have carried on my private passion for climbing. I have climbed oaks, bays and firs in the San Francisco bay area, junipers near Lake Tahoe, sequoias in the Sierras, hemlock in the Oregon Cascades, pine in the old Caledonian forest of Scotland. Some years ago I decided never again to cut a Christmas tree. I made up my own holiday tradition. Because my birthday is Christmas Day, I chose to give myself a gift every December 25th by finding a tree to climb. Up there I renew my gratefulness for Life. I become the ornament! And, most importantly, I become a student of what Wise Old Nature has to teach.

The other day I carried on my tradition, ascending a scented cedar on a friend's farm here on the island. Today, I want to pass along some of what I was reminded of, 60 feet up in that Great Teacher. Some of the lessons I learn are private and personal, but I think it's o.k. to let you in on *Six of the Top Lessons*—the Top lessons, so to speak.

First Lesson from a treetop: It takes a choosing, an effort, risk, to get a new perspective sometimes. You may have to sweat and get sappy hands. You may have to push through obstacles right in your face and get sticks and webs in your hair and beard. This first lesson is something John Muir and Henry Thoreau reminded us of. Choose to immerse in Nature and see things differently, view the world from an unusual or unexpected vantage point. This takes work, risk and a desire to learn more about this wonderful world that we are part of, intimately interrelated with. Margaret Fuller extolled this first lesson when she wrote describing the meeting of land and water: "a new creation takes place beneath the eye" (*Meditations of Margaret Fuller*, selection 38). The first lesson, simply put, is that there are lessons to be blessed with—if we but choose to be students, to take the effort to climb, to see.

The Second Lesson is like unto the first: Up there it isn't so much about seeing farther, it's about seeing what's right at hand, literally, at and on your hands. Sure it's nice to be able to look around the forest, watch the wind blowing in other trees, or see the distant horizon. Yet, it's a deeper art really, to catch sight of what is right before us. With the eyes to see, the ears to hear. I find tiny bugs, beetles I've never seen. I discover odd growths and twisted branches not seen from down below. Thoreau once found a blossom high up there and took it into town. No one could identify the flower though they spent their entire lives walking under those trees. As a chaplain among unsheltered people for many years (people who often lived in the sheltering forest) I constantly had to re-align my sight—to face the unfaceable faces of those who are rejected by our communities—to see my own face, and a "divine" face perhaps, in each person seeking an elusive thing called home. It's not about seeing farther, it's about seeing deeper—or higher, as the case may be. Once, high in a fir in Northern California, I realized that I was seeing what no one would *ever* see; that 99% of what lives and dies on this planet will *never* be seen by any human being! I learned that lesson among our society's poor as well. I find that humbling, don't you? A great call and challenge. Doesn't it make you want to be an explorer, a climber, at least a heretic?

The Third Lesson is precarious: It's about balance. Balance is critically important. When in a tree you have to respect where you are. It can be dangerous to space out! I'm not talking about having a tight grip. I'm talking about holding yourself in a balanced manner where you can even let go and be safe. The third lesson is both reasonable and intuitive. It's the honest response to all these natural disasters the world is facing. Where do we build our communities and are we building wisely, in balance with Nature's Way? It's not about keeping a tight grip on all the stuff we value. It's about living with the land and the sea with a clear, common sense. Living harmoniously with Nature, we see the branches of the issues—but we simultaneously see the roots. We learn to respect where we are. Balance is precarious, but it's pretty much everything.

Moving along to **the Fourth Lesson:** There are lots of trees in the forest, many species of trees, and many forests on the earth to learn lessons in. Steinbeck once wrote that his sons grew up thinking there was only one river, the one they enjoyed in youth. But they would one day find out that "there are other rivers." There are other trees too. You can have a favorite. You may choose to have a preference. Fine. Just remember: there are others to choose from and countless lessons to learn from them. A bit like Religion wouldn't you say? Perhaps we have our favorite and we sit comfortably in it. But what if we climbed through the branches of another tradition for awhile? Or, more radically, rootedly, let go of all we've been handed by history and try our own hand—make our own ascent. The fourth lesson is the heretical way; yet it is the interfaith way, the interspecies way, the honest and meaningful way, and the pioneering path of letting go of the exclusive branches we cling to. This lesson rings true: There are other trees, other forests.

The Fifth Lesson has to do with Fear: This is related to balance, risk. Yet it's more. When you are in the top of a tree (and I mean *in*, not on) you can feel the breezes, the winds, changes in temperature, in ways you can't always feel on the ground. In fact, you can't always even see the ground from above. You have to be fearless—or at least fully aware of your fear—, as well as self-reliant, grounded within, while being cautious, alert, aware, awake. Good and wise guidelines. Isn't this one lesson we need to hear and practice most in our World of Fear today? The fifth lesson is a timely reminder: Never be ruled by Fear.

The Sixth Lesson is the last I'll share with you today. It is related to the others because these are all interrelated instructions from the curriculum of the cedar. The sixth tree-text reads like this: Up high you feel a circular motion as the tree sways from the roots to the tip where you sit; *All Things move in a circle* because we live on a circle that spins on a circular axis through a circular, elliptical orbit around a fiery solar circle. Black Elk's vision of the hoops of the world interconnecting is part of this lesson. And Emerson's wonderful essay on "Circles" expresses it well. Emerson wrote, "The eye is the first circle; the horizon which it forms is the second; and throughout nature this primary figure is repeated without end. It is the highest emblem in the cipher of the world ... Our life is an apprenticeship to the truth that around every circle another can be drawn; that there is no end in nature, but every end is a beginning." Thank you Waldo.

I know why Muir called you "a Sequoia." The sixth lesson is clear: We are all, on this spinning planet, included in the one great circle of creation. We are people of the Circle. Thus the trees teach.

2007

7

A Radical Religion of Beauty

"The mountains are fountains of humanity as well as of rivers, of glaciers, of fertile soil. The great poets, philosophers, prophets, able people whose thoughts and deeds have moved the world, have come down from the mountains—mountain-dwellers who have grown strong there with the forest trees in Nature's workshops."
~John Muir, Alaska Journal, June-July, 1890

Originally published in The Humanist, *January-February, 2020*

I had already begun my pilgrimage out of faith, preparing to leave the ministry, when I decided to make another kind of pilgrimage back to Scotland and the boyhood home of the great naturalist John Muir in Dunbar, near Edinburgh. I had read *The Mountains of California* while snowshoeing in Hope Valley above Lake Tahoe and thumbed through his Journals like secular scripture while climbing trees in the watershed near my home across the bay from San Francisco. I was converted to Muir's worldview — his fundamentally humanist philosophy rooted in Nature.

Collecting salient selections from his writings into a little book of "meditations" I read them at his family home in Martinez, CA, at the Sierra Club's LeConte Lodge in Yosemite Valley and, at the invitation of the chief park ranger, under the magnificent cathedral of redwoods in Muir Woods National Monument. Later I penned a novella imagining the wondering naturalist meeting a youthful, wandering Nazarene.

The question I'm asking now is whether we might consider John Muir one of our humanist heroes, or even a "secular saint."

"Wildness is a necessity," the Sierra Sage wrote in 1901, on the first page of *Our National Parks*. We need wildness. We are creatures of wilderness— though we deny it, fear it. Thoreau had famously written, "In Wildness is the preservation of the World" (*Walking*). Muir took this a step further, literally. He took his mentor's statement as a map, since the Wiseman of Walden prefaced his famous words with "The West ... is but another name for the Wild." Muir turned his face to the Western mountains and discovered a radical religion-beyond-religion in the "fountains of humanity."

Throughout my own years of religious study, I read saints, mystics, theologians, biblical scholars, philosophers—digging around for wisdom wherever I might find it. As an ordained minister and chaplain I taught classes in churches on world religions, sacred scriptures and wisdom teachers across the spiritual landscape, reading delightful stories from Hasidic Jews and Sufi Muslims, Zen Buddhists and Native Americans, Native Africans, Catholic and Protestant Christians and more.

Then, out of the wilderness, the bearded and bewitching John Muir sauntered down the trail ("saunter," as Thoreau defined it, is a deep walking through the "holy land"—and all land is reverenced by a saunterer). Muir didn't "hike"—he sauntered.

Muir understood that religion, like humanity itself, too often fears the wild where it originated. With dry tea, a chunk of bread and curiosity in his pockets, John Muir fearlessly entered the wildness and emerged from the wilderness like Moses from Sinai, Buddha from the Indian forest, Jesus from the Judean desert, Muhammad from the Arabian cave (and like Galileo from his telescope or Darwin from his microscope). Yet—and this is crucially important—Muir was no prophet calling "Come unto Me." *His secular gospel was "Go" not "Come."* In essence he shouted, "Go saunter for yourself into the Great Classroom—the Greatest Temple!"

Akin to classic prophetic traditions he called for us to have an awakening, to leave our heavy theologies and holy books, to lighten our packs and risk an unpredictable journey, a challenging adventure. He pounded the pine-scented pulpit or lichen-laced lecturn: "Go!"!

Muir is remembered, appropriately, as the patriarchal parent of our National Parks; first president of the

Sierra Club; mountaineer; explorer and expert on glaciers. As his writings brought him fame and influence he slept in the snow under the stars with President Teddy Roosevelt, sailed in Alaskan fjords with fellow naturalist John Burroughs and fought a political fight to preserve wilderness like his treasured Hetch Hetchy Valley. He was much more than a "conservationist." The earth is not something to conserve— to "use" as a "resource"— but our home to *preserve*. He was a preservationist. "Keep Wilderness Wild" would be his bumpersticker—if he drove … if he had a car.

When I initially read *My First Summer in the Sierra*, I thought: this sounds almost like mysticism, some ancient saint or sage—it sounds almost "spiritual" without being preachy. He's describing our world, fully accessible to me, to anyone, and I know what he says is true because I've been there! Hiking in Yosemite, snowshoeing among the ancient sequoias and gnarled junipers, you can breathe in the alpine air and touch the same trees, delighting in the same wildflowers and granite crags he did. Standing in the refreshing mist of cool cascades, Muir seems present in the mists of time. It's as if he's on the trail beside us, teaching at every step in the open-air classroom.

Unlike Moses, he descended from a mountaintop only to be a secular evangelist—a naturalistic preacher—crying: "Go out and hear, see, sense the wildly good news of Nature!" As a good scientist, Muir welcomes verification of what he experiences (we have no record of anyone going out to verify the stories of Faith's Founders).

My First Summer in the Sierra, published in 1911, still has an almost scriptural resonance to it. On a hot July day above Yosemite Valley he scribbles in his tea-stained journal:

"Every hidden cell is throbbing with music and life, every fibre thrilling like harp strings, while incense is ever flowing from the balsam bells and leaves. No wonder the hills and groves were God's first temples, and the more they are cut down and hewn into cathedrals and churches, the farther off and dimmer seems the Lord himself. The same may be said of stone temples."

Every cell pulsates with life in Muir's congregation; every hill and forest is a temple. How do you manage that? How do you ritualize, dogmatize or creedalize Nature? With a leap of joy rather than a leap of faith he's ascended above the clouds of orthodoxy to discover the bubbling, babbling springs of humanity.

When he has a strange experience in the mountains, sensing the presence of a professor from his University of Wisconsin days in the valley below, he runs down to find his kindly teacher on the trail! Reflecting on this unusual event he writes:

"It seems supernatural, but only because it is not understood. Anyhow, it seems silly to make so much of it, while the natural and common is more truly marvelous and mysterious than the so-called supernatural. Indeed most of the miracles we hear of are infinitely less wonderful

than the commonest of natural phenomena, when fairly seen."

This reasonable, common sense response is strong evidence for Muir's natural humanistic perspective. His innate skepticism is time and again revealed in a careful choice of words, though he often uses religious terms familiar to his readers.

He still speaks of God, for instance, yet what have the mountains taught him? Not that an invisible deity is commanding obedience from burning trees. And certainly not that a strict father in the sky is killing his own child on a bloody tree for his own satisfaction. There's nothing natural about any of that.

Muir's Lord is absolutely visible, revealed in the creative forces of nature. Is this pure Pantheism? Perhaps. But I think more. His divinity is palpable, incarnate as rain, ice, fire, wind, actively sculpting and creating an evolving earth. *Yes, Nature and God are one, yet beyond anthropomorphic representation or anthropocentric hubris.*

How do we begin to understand Muir's Nature-God? In one of the most significant entries in his journals Muir asserts this heretical belief: "No synonym for God is so perfect as Beauty" (June, 1875). This is seminal, central, essential in understanding Muir's use of religious terminology minus the theological stickiness. In another journal entry he exclaims: "Oh, the infinite abundance and universality of Beauty. Beauty is God. What shall we say of God, that we may not say of Beauty!" (quoted in Linnie Marsh Wolfe, *Son of the Wilderness*). Let any concept of "God" slip away; Beauty is the incarnation of the cosmos minus any transcendence diverting attention to a more beautiful world that simply doesn't exist and doesn't need to.

Consider his view of the Bible. He respects the ancient book, but he discovered much more ancient pages to read, sculpted in stone by glaciers. He speaks of "Nature's Bible" written in the mountain ranges, especially in Alaska and his beloved "Range of Light," the Sierra Nevada.

As a boy in Scotland, John's evangelist father forced him to memorize large portions of the Bible. He always carried that book in his brain, but he carried Robert Burns in his heart, singing the poet's ballads to squirrels and birds in the highlands of California and beyond.

"Wildly here, without control, Nature reigns and rules the whole," wrote Burns, his beloved Scottish kinsman ("Castle Gordon"). And so Muir rooted his sauntering faith in this-world and no other. His oft-repeated exclamation, "Glorious!," was not directed to deity but to the uncontrollable creations of Lord Nature.

In Kristin Wintermute's excellent article on the "Ten Commitments" (*The Humanist*, August 2019), she neatly summarizes Humanism's environmental concern: "Humanity is also capable of positive environmental change that values the interdependence of all life on this planet." A hopeful, practical, inclusive vision shared by John of the Mountains who wrote:

"The universe would be incomplete without [humankind]; but it would also be incomplete without the smallest transmicroscopic creature that dwells beyond our conceitful eyes and knowledge" (*A Thousand-Mile Walk to the Gulf*, 1916). .

What does our adopted humanist think of sermons and lectures? Education was paramount for this dropout from the University of Wisconsin, but so was active participation—deep involvement in the world. Who are the primary professors? Those with feathers, fur and fins. *Muir's clergy have wings; his seminary is a sequoia.* Grasshoppers deliver sermons on granite pulpits; hawks offer seminars.

What does he say about Religion itself? How organized can faith be, when we are born and baptized in wildness? True religion cannot be found in the artificial "houses of god." A wide-open, heretical and humanistic religion is not found in books, beliefs, dogmas, doctrines or confessions. He proclaims, in agreement with his friend and fellow naturalist John Burroughs, that a living religion (belief system, worldview) cannot be centered in theology at all.

Maybe the religious world is not ready for that? If not, humanists and naturalists will gladly lead the way, and Muir is near the front of the pack guiding us forward.

What does Muir say about Heaven? That's fairly simple. We're already there; it's already here. Not a perfect paradise, but garden enough. Nothing supernatural about it at all.

Does Muir's universe have a Hell? He once said that if hell is a dark, rocky pit, he'd climb right out of it! We, all by ourselves, create something hellish when we bring suffering on our fellow inhabitants on the spinning—and warming— globe. Nature makes heaven; we make hell.

Muir's radical faith is both sensible and sapient: faith is rational, heuristic pleasure in the wonder of the world. Nothing more, nothing less.

Finally, *what does he say about church* (or any sacred place)? This is a solitary or social direct experience with wilderness, where the wild things are the congregation and we are the ones who must join, not they. A wildness found deep in a national park or in our own neighborhood.

He climbs Cathedral Peak in the Sierras and testifies:

"This I may say is the first time I have been at church in California, led here at last, every door graciously opened for the poor lonely worshiper. In our best times everything turns into religion, all the world seems a church and the mountains altars." (My First Summer in the Sierra)

He blows the doors off any traditional sanctuary. No church, no sacred place, no religion is large enough to contain his wild worldview.

Where our secular saint leads us could be a new kind of Natural Religion, or even a religion beyond religion, deeper or higher than religion—maybe the roots of any true, relevant, perennial religion. Or, and I doubt he would be very shocked, to the end of anything we've known as religion.

His ecstatic celebration of Nature sounds almost like prayer or meditation:

"One is constantly reminded of the infinite lavishness and fertility of Nature—inexhaustible abundance amid what seems enormous waste. And yet when we look into any of her operations that lie within reach of our minds, we learn that no particle of her material is wasted or worn out. It is eternally flowing from use to use, beauty to yet higher beauty; and we soon cease to lament waste and death, and rather rejoice and exult in the imperishable, unspendable wealth of the universe, and faithfully watch and wait the reappearance of everything that melts and fades and dies about us, feeling sure that its next appearance will be better and more beautiful than the last."

"Beauty to yet higher beauty." Have you ever heard a more secular celebration of life?

Muir's curiosity was contagious:

"How interesting everything is! Every rock, mountain, stream, plant, lake, lawn, forest, garden, bird, beast, insect seems to call and invite us to come and learn something of its history and relationship. But shall the poor

ignorant scholar be allowed to try the lessons they offer? It seems too great and good to be true."

This enthusiasm for the natural classroom, an exuberance he shared with Darwin, Humboldt, Thoreau, Rachel Carson, Jane Goodall, E.O. Wilson, Neil deGrasse Tyson and other like-minded tramp-arounds, was the major reason Muir wasn't distracted by supernatural side-trails. The natural was super enough, good enough, the world was full of God/Beauty. Why invent something artificial, inferior, when Beauty is eternally present.

John Muir reminds us that all things—like us—are permeated with Wild. Wilderness is a sacred sanctuary, essential for us. The wild places are temples and cathedrals, churches, synagogues, mosques and zendos. And ... they are so much more.

Religion, wild or tamed, is a valuable study. We must be religiously literate in our wildly religious world. And, as I see it, it's a subject best taught by humanists in a secular context, especially in Nature, to see what survives in the open air and sunlight.

To directly address our critical environmental crises today, we need Muir to remind us of two essentials to pack along: first, we have to meet on common ground (say a city, state or national park), focused on the beauty at hand, regardless of our divisive views. And second, it's not just about beauty.

Writing to his sister Sarah in 1873, Muir writes the

words we find emblazoned on t-shirts and posters: "The mountains are calling and I must go." Yet he follows this with: "And I will work on while I can, studying incessantly." Beauty is not merely for recreation and contemplation, it is an invitation to learn more, conserve more, preserve more. This takes devoted work and study.

As Muir's close friend Robert Underwood Johnson wrote after Muir's death, "[People] will search for beauty as scientists search for truth, knowing that while truth can make one free, it is beauty of some sort ... that alone can give permanent happiness" (American Academy of Arts and Letters, New York, 1916). Preserving wild spaces is preserving the beauty, and ourselves.

I see this as one reason Muir would be a leader in presenting solutions to our climate crisis. He would identify it as a consciousness crisis first, then entice us into the beauty, both the marred and the marvelous, demanding we "work on; study incessantly."

Our naturally humanist hero once stood in the pristine paradise of Alaska and exulted:

"When we contemplate the whole globe as one great dewdrop, striped and dotted with continents and islands, flying through space with other stars all singing and shining together as one, the whole universe appears as an infinite storm of beauty." (Travels in Alaska, 1915)

The whole tiny globe is like a drop of water spilling

through limitless space, one star among countless stars. And when we contemplate and contextualize this, what do we see? How do we feel? What is Humanity that anyone should be mindful of us? For Muir, and potentially for us, the universe presents itself as "an infinite storm of beauty." The "call" and "mission" is to learn from the storms whether destructive or creative; to better understand our world and be wiser participants in the grand show.

John Muir's radical Religion of Beauty, stirring education, environmental action as well as awe-inspiring emotional connection to all things earth, may serve to be the most natural bridge for humanists and religionists to explore. Though most of us have left the god-language behind, we can appreciate the trailblazing work of Muir to point us toward something more profound and practical than any religion has ever been.

If the wild Scotsman was correct, that "wildness is a necessity," that "mountains are fountains of life," then going out and up is our best hope for a humanistic future. Muir's "gospel of beauty" represents the essence of humanism's goals, and we don't have to be mountain-climbers (or have bushy beards) to saunter in his footsteps, and beyond.

2019

8

Natural Economics

"There are days when the field water and the slender grasses and the wild hawks have it all over the rest of us."
~Mary Oliver, "Gratitude"

Economy and environment. These two words are all over our eyes and minds today. But do we realize just how related they are? I remember the word *oikos* from my Greek class in college. It's where we get the prefix *eco* and it originally meant "house" or "household." Talk about your house—that's ecology. Say something about the whole inhabited world—that's ecumenical. Get into a discussion about responsible management of your household, or the household of the community—that's economy. Open the doors of the household and you find the environs—the circle that surrounds. In this sense, everyone—by Nature—is an environmentalist. But how do we manage the circular household that surrounds us when we don't even think about the fact that it is a house and this house has an intricate and intimate relationship to all other houses, including the dens and nests, oceans and forests and skies?

The interrelatedness and connectedness of our common dwellings make more sense the deeper we dig into these words and the realities behind them. What happens on Wall Street doesn't only affect Main Street but the deer-trails and duck paddles, the wildebeest and whale migration routes. The great money games and whatever recessions, depressions and stimulating piles of cash and credit have a vast impact on our lives and the national and global households. Chickasaw writer Linda Hogan, in her book *Dwellings*, says: "I write out of respect for the natural world, recognizing that humankind is not separate from nature." When will we wake up to see that our economy is simply everything we do and everything we do touches everything else? It is simply too ignorant and even dangerous in today's world to fight over land and homes and national borders when in reality—in reality—there is only one neighborhood, one home. That's a truth we can take to the bank and cash.

While I held the position of Adjunct Instructor, I taught a class at Dominican University of California I titled:" The Green God: Paths toward a New Environmental Creed." I led students on a journey with two "housekeepers"—John of the Mountains and Trees (Muir) and John of the Rivers and Birds (Burroughs). These thinkers and writers were earthshaking contributors to a revolutionary form of natural economics. We are all their students in the great classroom circle of Nature and who knows what might happen, if in the current economic meltdown, more of us turned to the lessons of the household, to better manage the house, to allow the house and its diverse inhabitants to better manage us?

We're in need of a new ethic, a new creed, a new "god" if you use that language, cleaning the house of our minds and communities, building new innovative models of one great compassionate community with an enthusiastic, evangelistic commitment to radical biomimicry—learning Nature's fundamental lessons. As a teacher, writer and "earth chaplain" (in a caring relationship with Nature) I do not say these things lightly but pragmatically.

We need a new open door, a warm welcoming, to this ancient home renewing itself along with us everyday. Perhaps our commerce and sense of genuine community directly depend upon the level of respect we practice in the household; perhaps we could consider taking our shoes off. We're all related here. Yes, the bear sleeps on the couch and the hawk sits on the lamp, the otter splashes in the sink and the wolf curls around your feet. Live with it. It's their home too. Doesn't this sound both logical and eco-logical to you?

2009

9

Life is Too Short

*"To simplify one's life! It seems the most natural
thing in the world to undertake, yet it's
just about the most difficult."*
~Henry Miller, Big Sur

Another weekend's sleep-in was interrupted by a neighbor's dog barking in their yard down the street. Living in the forest is fine, and wild creatures give it a remote feeling, but domestic animals can take something from the experience. After about an hour and a half of nearly nonstop arrffing and yowling I picked up my weapon of choice, turning it over in my hands. It felt good on my skin —sleek, smooth, strong and sharp—ready to send a message clear and cutting ... my pen. Not a weapon to use against the animal, mind you. I like some dogs. Really. It's unmindful, untamed, unneighborly neighbors I have difficulty with. It's them I feel like attacking with this most powerful of weapons. So I began to write on the small, blue legal pad:

"Awakening to a morning's bark (alas, not of the tree kind)   . . .bark, bark, bark. Then more, bark, Bark,

bark and the finale (a finale that never ends): Bark, Bark, Bark!" I signed it, "Your neighbor, who will, next time, bark at the cops."

This was the second time in as many months that I'd sauntered a poetic scribbling down the hill and artfully placed the paper in a tree limb by the neighbor's garage door. I don't like confrontation anyway (though my entire career as a counselor belies that) so it felt good to make my creative statement and smile as I walked back up, all the while knowing that the owners ("masters"!) would likely not return until much later in the day. When my nearer neighbor rode up on his bike saying "Can you *believe* it?," with a nod toward the dog-house, complaining that he and his partner had suffered with the noise all morning, I took him back and read him my poem-grenade. He laughed and exclaimed, "That's great. Much better than what I planned to do!"

Reminding others to be mindfully awake and aware has been unfortunately tied into my work for many years. Not because I'm necessarily more awake and aware; it simply seems, at times, I'm more aware that I am unaware, comparatively speaking, day in and year out. Early Sunday School lessons, a slathering of Jewish ethics and later Buddhist and Taoist lessons put a certain responsibility in my face and in my lap. I'm *free* to do as I please, not judged by the Universe, yet I'm also *responsible*, to myself, others and that greater One, Nature (as Viktor Frankl once said, there should be a Statue of Responsibility on the West Coast to balance the Statue of Liberty on the East).

What I choose to do responds to my environment and co-responds to the "greater purpose of compassion." Or so I would hope. As an interfaith chaplain in three incarnations—as a teacher with people who are labeled disabled, as a jail chaplain locked in with offenders and, for ten years, serving as street chaplain among houseless people in one of the richest counties in America—I had to respond with corresponding compassion to crisis after crisis as counselor, spiritual guide, teacher and friend. I've had to stay wide awake. . .and bark at the nonsense.

When my father died in 1984, followed by my mother in 1991, I began to radically alter my perception of Life. My father had spoken of retirement, preparing for years to take all those fishing trips he'd dreamed of. The year he retired, after 30 years at Boeing, cancer snuck up and strangled him and all that was left was fishing gear in the closet. Mom outlived him a little, having battled arthritis for as far back as I can remember, planning more of her world journeys to see what's out there. But, ol 'demon cancer stabbed her too, and she went down with discomfort mixed with dignity—slipping off into a morphine sleep as I sat vigil. It's not quite enough to say their deaths simply altered my perceptions. When they left, or rather, altered their presence, a deeply abiding new sense sunk into all I am, all I do and say. This sense can only be described with words as *Life is too short.*

More than a mantra, this brief brush of wisdom's brush not only came to guide me; it became and still becomes the single principle upon which Life's fragility totters.

What I mean particularly by "Life is too short" is not exactly a complaint. I'm not saying "Shit! This life is so short and it ought to be longer. I'd make it different, and better!" What I'm thinking with this short line is that I now profoundly recognize the brevity of this bodily presence we call living and seek to guide my life by something more than "Oh, I have all the time in the world," or "I'll wait and do that wonderful thing later," or "This or that matters so much that I can't live without it," or, this may be the biggest, "I've got to hold on tight to this thing or this person because I don't want to lose it/them." Call it a sense of transience, impermanence, or whatever. I know, deep in heart and mind, that life is a flash, a spark, a shooting star, a wave of the sea. . .something quick, often painful, often wonderful and beautiful and therefore incredibly, no!—credibly precious. I can believe in Life because of its immense worth. And I think I'm a better, more balanced person since I face it squarely and honestly and wholeheartedly as "short."

Seeking to guide one's life by a cognizance of life's shortness may actually be a manner of conducting life by an open attitude of "Life is too short to *not* do, to *not* say or experience" something. Does this necessitate a fearful reaction that "anything goes?" The moralistic pious would perhaps have that reaction. Are there limits or boundaries to this freeing attitude to live one's life by an open principle of "What if?" What if I stopped working so much and took more time to enjoy the leisure side of life? What if I let go of the turbulent stream of contemporary life, swam out of the torrent and contemplated the beauty of things more? Are there places I've always wanted to go, things or people I desire to see, experiences I've wished to have, books I've dreamed of reading or writing? All these challenging questions urge me not to let it pass—the experience or this short life. The boundaries are mutable and often moot. So am I, so is my so-called life.

Life's tragedies have a sculpting influence on these matters. As Bertrand Russell once wrote, *"In these moments of insight [marked by pain, suffering and mystery], we lose all eagerness of temporary desire, all struggling and striving for petty ends, all care for the little trivial things that, to a superficial view, make up the common life of day by day; we see, surrounding the narrow raft illumined by the flickering light of human comradeship, the dark ocean on whose rolling waves we toss for a brief hour. . ."* (*A Free Man's Worship*, 1903). Our darkest times bring us into the liminal moments that shape us, though tossed on the waves like driftwood. The trivial, the flickering and rolling, can serve to jar us awake to the meaning of our existence in the sharpest moments of sight or insight. Russell is expounding a truth I now live by. Pain, loss, suffering of all kinds will happen. No avoiding possible. Yet, as a Native American man on the street once said to me in a conversation about principles of living: "All I can do is my best." I responded, "Life is too short to *not* do our best."

Another channel that this river could swirl down would be the one where a person could say: "Life is so short; I'm going to live it to the hilt and risk it all in dangerous adventure." This can be seen in those who enjoy "death-defying feats" of thrill, those who push the limits of endurance and safety in extreme sports or practice sexual conquests. Interestingly enough this careless attitude is also evident in those who believe in a religious fundamentalism that preaches: "This life is short and sinful so we don't care if we die; there's a better Eternal life ahead, beyond death, so let's be martyrs for heaven." I will only say here that this sad devaluation of the earth and the body is not what I personally mean when I realize the brevity of the life span. This thundering cascade of the moment dries up while it loses the wonderful, priceless treasure of beauty that is life itself.

Far from a complaint, excuse or reckless abandon, this abiding, guiding principle presents me with a life full of opportunity to explore, discover, invent, be real and honest, and to live as *I Must Live*, by choice, by my own gifts and abilities. To practice a Short Life is tantamount to setting sail to new lands or even planets, not to be a self-styled adventurer or brash jock of a journeyer but to learn, grow, be awestruck and stunned by what lies out in the vast world around, even within.

Life is *not* too short (for most of us) to see, hear, feel or think something new, create something innovative, be a better person or go where no one has gone before (thank you, *Star Trek*). Life is *not* too short to condense the best of what life offers into one's own span of experience. It might mean some sacrifice of myths of success and stability to achieve a balance of simplicity and comfort, or at least contentment. Choosing to live a short life may entail some harsh realism blended, one could hope, with an equal amount of playfulness, humor and intrinsic joy. I've seen this in some who have terminal diseases, who find a way to exude a sifting of goodheartedness (without that killer, bitterness) and a gutsy humor in the face of obvious pain and even a little fear.

I've felt this when conducting a memorial service for a baby who suffered for many months as his parents tried desperate procedures to keep him alive. At the service, the mother was just as interested and focused on making lemonade for everyone who came, with a smile and a hug for each, as she was in telling us how she had to say goodbye and let her little one go. Her gesture of release, raising her hands and throwing her arms apart, became our corporate ritual of grieving—a gift to us. The father, without I think denying his pain at all, had smiles and gratefulness to give to each person.

Life indeed is not too short to love, to be kind, to struggle for grace and peace, to create and to give. It is up to us, and we ought to choose this—the best of ways to live, because there is precious little time to waste.

Henry Thoreau once wrote a poem that contained the line, "Think on thy home, my soul, and think aright, of what's yet left thee of life's wasting day." Having read a great deal of the Concord naturalist's writing I would not conclude that he was thinking necessarily of some heaven beyond. In light of the fact that this was the man who wrote "heaven is under our feet as well as over our heads" I can only surmise that his sense of "home" was life lived to the fullest and best here and now, in what the poet Rumi so gently and eloquently described as, this. . . branching. . . present. . .moment (are you breathing now?).

2003

10

By the Hands of Nature

I gave this talk as a member of the Speakers' Bureau of the national Secular Student Alliance, during "Earth Week" at Cabrillo College, Aptos, CA

I'm honored to be a part of this week when we celebrate the big blue, soggy rock spinning in space, the chunk of the cosmos we call home (and ought to treat as a reverenced residence).

Biologists tell us a startling fact: our bodies contain hundreds of millions of bacteria cells, which comes out to more bacteria cells than human cells! So, I want to welcome all you *colonies of bacteria* here today. This is definitely the largest audience I've ever spoken to! But even that's a little more polite than what an alien said to the *Enterprise* crew on *Star Trek*, when it called them "ugly bags of mostly water." Well, when you think about it, that's a pretty accurate description.

So, here we are. Bags of watery bacteria. As an old Philosophy Professor used to say: "Go and think about that, for ten or twenty years!" Seriously, I'm grateful for the invitation to speak this afternoon. I'm a strong supporter of the Secular Student Alliance and I've donated copies of my book, *Life After Faith* (re-published as *From Faith to Freethought*) to the National organization and to Sonya, their representative here. Back in my conservative Christian days, the word *secular* made us shake and pray and run to hide behind our big black bibles. Then I came to understand that *secular*, in my simplistic way of thinking, simply means "this present world." I can't honestly speak about any other world. What better way to address concerns about the world we share and celebrate our small rocky, watery home on this place we call Earth, than to speak of secular—down to earth—things?

This week, in April 1838, a child was born in Dunbar, Scotland, who would give the world National Parks, a new understanding of how the earth was created, cut and sculpted by glaciers, and maybe, just maybe, he helped build a bridge beyond belief, beyond our irrational and UN-earthly beliefs. I've always felt Muir's presence in the mountains. Especially when I was walking somewhere he described in his books or journals. On my second trip to Scotland, I sensed him even more. . .or at least I felt I *understood* him better. *Meditations of John Muir*, my first book, came out just after my Scottish pilgrimage. Muir became for me a kind of Natural Saint. A spiritual teacher who helped me completely re-interpret what "Spirituality" means.

This last weekend my wife and I were walking around the lakes of the Marin County Watershed. We saw a line of turtles sunning themselves on some logs and then noticed a trio of young boys catching lizards. One of them started throwing stones at the turtles and we yelled across at them. Their father was standing nearby, not saying anything, but talking on his cell-phone. We walked away shaking our heads. Such a disconnect we have from Nature. And it starts with the children.

A few years ago I was living in a one-room cabin in the forest on a Northwest island. I was invited to speak to a High School class so I took the students along a path into the woods surrounding the school and read a few selections from my Muir book. Along the way we stopped in a small grove of fir and hemlock and I asked the class to bend down and scoop a bit of dirt in their hands. As you might expect, some of them refused, "Oooo. I'm not getting my hands DIRTY!" It took some coaxing before they would even *touch the ground* under their feet. I guess that was all the Muir they could handle, literally, that day!

Well, some may be afraid to get their hands dirty, but I wonder, Why is it people are still so drawn to the Muddy Guy Muir, perhaps even more than dirty old Thoreau? There's something about this wild Scottish fool who tramped all over the planet, that makes us want to hike around with him (even in our *heads*). We want to see some of those incredible, unbelievable things he saw and sink into those earthy (secular) experiences. But to do that, we have to be converted to a kind of *bio-degradable Religion*, a bio-mimicking Science and *Bio* itself. . .LIFE as a journey of endless, joyful delight. . .muddy and mucked up as it can be. Muir talks *dirty* to us and we love it!

John Muir sauntered his way through life in the wild spaces—*saunter* is a great Thoreauvian word: to feel at home with the earth, to walk deeply, mindfully—Muir sauntered, full of deep curiosity and delight, across vast distances. During his 1000-mile walk from Indiana to the Gulf of Mexico in 1867 he described the Cumberland Mountains and green, forested valleys of Kentucky as "an Eden" abundant with a "paradise of oaks." He said the "glorious forest road" stretched over the hills and valleys, the path molded and curved *"by the hands of Nature."* Being John Muir, he couldn't help himself, saying, he was sauntering through "the most sublime and comprehensive picture that ever entered" his eyes. He stepped into the painting, the art of Eden, of masterwork of Earth.

Muir was a playful and punning artist with words (he liked to sketch too). . .and he was the *ultimate, sustainable secularist.* His only interest was in "this present world"—this down-to-the-ground and up-to-the-mountains kind of real world where Nature is all and everything and fully, completely *enough.* Confucius was once asked to comment on spiritual beings and the other world. The old sage replied, "If we're not yet able to serve people, how can we serve spiritual beings; if we know so little about life, how can we say anything about death or the afterlife." (*Analects,* 11:11). Confucius and Muir would have made good camping companions!

Raised by a strict Christian father, Muir knew the Bible inside and out, front to back, upside down and backwards (my own evangelical background injected me with the same kind of bible-in-the-blood). He once said if hell was a deep pit, he would simply find the handholds and footholds and climb (the hell) out! (my paraphrase). Like Muir, those of us born and raised as believers, our brains baked with bible passages, "pray" for nothing more than to be "saved" from spirituality, to climb out of restrictive, confining thinking and immerse ourselves in the freethinking, fresh air and liberating baptisms of *this* world, the only world we know, full of Nature's wide-open beauty.

This line, "By the hands of Nature" is very instructive. . .a good introduction to Muir's healthy use of rich anthropomorphisms. We have to be careful here because I think this is one reason Muir is so misunderstood by folks who paint him as a Good Christian. Much of the picturesque language Muir uses in his literature is drawn from humanity to express what is immensely greater than humanity. The reference point is the Human Species. . .and the more we venture and discover the more we see there are countless, limitless reference points. Of course, we love re-creating the world in Our Image! As an old religion prof said to us, "God made us in God's Image. . .and we've returned the favor ever since!" We create our Gods. . .other worlds, other realities. That's coming from a theological perspective of course. But what if we looked at the world differently? As Muir said, see the world with our "heads upside down?" The hands of Nature, the heart of Nature, the head of Nature, the body of Nature. . .it all speaks of our need to use the language we know and understand to express and explain what we don't know and don't understand. And so it is with faith and religion, myth and fantasy, dreams and hopes and human wonder. We put our face on the wonder and beauty and mystery and *in-credibleness* of Nature. . .and we want to believe. . .to believe ultimately in all of it, and perhaps, more than anything, to believe in ourselves. Nothing really "wrong" with that; we just need to admit it.

And here is where the bushy-bearded Scotsman leaps into the conversation. Muir offers one steady log set across the turbulent confluence of science and faith, philosophy and theology, culture and government—all of it. His philosophy is not the only answer or solution for our disconnect from the great vibrating web of life, or our discontent with our minuscule place in it all. But Muir, along with his friend John Burroughs and Burroughs' friend Walt Whitman, may offer the best trail out of this boggy thicket of spiritualizing and super-naturalizing. We have lost our way with distractions. We need to find some traction to climb up, out and beyond these dead-end trails, these UN-imaginative distractions.

Muir's *faith-free religion* can easily be seen in his famous line:

"Climb the mountains and get their good tidings, Na-

ture's peace will flow into you. As the sunshine into the trees, the winds will blow their freshness into you. And the storms their energy, while cares will drop away like autumn leaves."

Highly charged spiritual language here. Muir was unashamed to utilize the ancient terminology and images he grew up with (good tidings, good news, gospel, peace and wind like a spirit with energized storms that blow away our cares and worries). Beautiful linguistics. And the reference point, the grounding for the language, is entirely natural, and, as I read him, utterly devoid of anything super-natural. If we asked Muir if he was a "believer" he would probably answer with an enthusiastic "Aye!" (Aye Lad. . .Aye Lass!). But what would he mean? He certainly used the word God and many other religious terms. Which might turn off many secularists and agitate many religious folks.

Yet, I would argue that his direct experience and participation in the natural world caused him to believe only in what he could put his hands and feet on, what he could grip and grasp, what he could touch and climb and smell and see in the great landscape of life.

So, what was Muir's *church*, what was his cathedral, synagogue, mosque? The mountain temples. What was his *scripture*? The torah, gospel, qur'an, dharma and endless scientific and philosophical lessons. . .all writ large, everywhere present in Nature. Texts written every moment of every day by rains and rivers, glaciers and winds, starfish and stars. . .and the tiniest tracks of grasshoppers, beetles, newts and slugs. His *congregation*? The trees and flowers and all wildlife. His *choir* music? The wind, the waterfalls and bird-songs. His *faith*? Well, that can be complicated, but I think he might say he felt Nature is "God's handiwork" and he believed in Nature's wisdom, Nature's creative acts, "Nature's peace will flow into you." More a Sense and an Experience than some leap of faith. Yes, leap from boulder to boulder, tree-limb to treelimb, but don't leap off a cliff! I think he put his faith, his trust, in Nature. It gave him delight.

Sometimes I say that Muir's kind of faith is simply, profoundly *delight*. . .overwhelming delight in the "glorious" world. The word *glorious* he used over and over, used to be reserved for God alone. For Mountain Man Muir, the whole earth was glorious! His *God*? Beauty (he said Beauty was the perfect synonym for God). . .the *Creator* of the Universe? Naturally, obviously, Nature. His *mission*? To entice us all to fearlessly live the delight, as a natural creature, one among a goo-gol (goo-GALL= ten raised to the power of one hundred) of glorious lifeforms; to reverence and respect all and to seek with all one's might to Conserve, Preserve, Celebrate and Participate in it all (I think at times environmentalists and scientists forget that to conserve and preserve isn't enough. . .Muir and his trekkers remind us to go farther. . .they don't want us to miss the glorious celebration, the grateful participation in the great community we call Cosmos). Without celebration and participation we'll just continue to *use* Nature for our purposes, even good sustainable purposes, to claim Nature for our programs, our recreation, or attempt to preserve it like some delicate display in a grand museum.

Muir's *religionless religion and faithless faith* are a breath of fresh air in the history of humanity's sense of awe, wonder and mystery. What do we do with our delight ... our WOW experiences? Think about the *evolution of religion*, the *origins of faith*:

Moses came down from the Sinai mountain of Egypt with commands cut in stone (so the story goes).

Muir says, Climb the mountains and read the messages in the stones and glaciers for yourself!

Jesus emerged from the desert wilderness of Palestine with a gospel linked to another world, a call to repentance, saying Come to Me.

Muir says, Go out to the wilderness; hear Nature's earth-shaking, earth-making message; every step is breaking news! Shake off the "sin" of the city and be cleansed by the wild earth; Don't believe me, You go! (Come *with* me, if you choose, but don't come *to* me-- this is about Nature, not old John Muir).

Buddha calmly walked out of the forests of India with a bow and breath of peace and a pack full of dharma saying Wake Up!

Muir says, Come to the woods for here is rest. . .going out is really going in. The sun shines not [just] on us but in us. The rivers flow not [just] past us but through us. When we are with Nature we are awake.

Muhammad went into an Arabian cave and came out as a tribal prophet of the One and Only and Best God.

Muir went to the Range of Light and proclaimed he was already in heaven, "I breathe the atmosphere of angels." The one and only God is Beauty!

Joseph Smith came out of his New York farm fields and said he had a new book, a new religion (and a new pair of gold sunglasses) to tell the world about, a new vision of heaven.

Muir says, In *these* fields a single day in so divine an atmosphere of beauty and love would be well worth living for. . .and immortal life beyond the grave is not essential to perfect happiness.

All the Mystics, Saints and "Spiritual Superstars & Superheroes" of all traditions across the globe have quietly pointed to the "Super" above and beyond and behind the Natural.

Muir ecstatically bounded into the unbounded wilds to yell a wake up call: *"As soon as we are absorbed in the*

*harmony—plain, mountain, calm, storm, lilies and se-
quoias, forests and [meadows] are only different strands
of many-colored Light--[they and we] are one in the sun-
beam!"* (Journal, 1872)

Most religions preach about love, compassion, justice
and struggle to sustain insular tribal communities
and to explain the details of death. Muir calmly says:
*"Nature loves [humanity], beetles and birds with the same
love. With her storms. . .she seems to scatter. . .death
among her creatures, and so she does, but they are scattered as the stars are scattered in the heavens. . .singing
together. . .Indeed every atom. . .is inspired with un-
changeable love."* (Journal, May, 1871)

It's fairly obvious that when Muir stumbled out of
the mountains, forests, meadows, deserts to tell his
fantastic stories, he didn't expect people to believe
him, believe *in* him or follow him and definitely not
to have disciples start some new Muirite Religion. He
said that he lived only to "entice" people to go out
there and see and explore and learn for themselves.
Now think about it: *Every one of those Religious Reb-
els left the Old Religion to offer something New.* But
then, something bizarre happened—not unexpected,
but bizarre. Have you ever thought how very odd it is
that the wild experiences in wide open nature of Religion's Founders immediately lead to building projects
—building boxes for the beliefs, packages for piety, sacred spaces enclosed and closed off for members only?

Strange, isn't it? Sanctuaries with doors and locks. *The*

uncontrollable imaginative experience occurs in a forest and the response is to cut the forest down to build a temple to worship the original experience and control all future experience. We humans are quite odd, aren't we? And of course, then millions more trees are destroyed to create holy icons and holy books so people can forever repeat the same stories over and over as they look out on a desecrated landscape.

For balance, think of all the people who crowd into exhibits, theaters and bookstores in Yellowstone, the Grand Canyon or any National Park fumbling with their digital cameras or scrambling for snacks and souvenirs right in the center of the Cathedral! Nature help us if we hear a loud cellphone ringing by a mountain stream!

Now, I've worked beside and lived with people of faith for a long time, and so did Muir. So, I'm not implying we disparage or discard all supernaturalists. In fact, I think it's critical to our world that believers and non-believers figure out creative new ways to get along, or the Earth will continue to suffer. It is possible; it must be possible.

I was an interfaith freethinking chaplain for a long while, then the director of a homeless shelter co-ordinating Evangelicals, Jews, Catholics, Protestants, Unitarians, agnostics, atheists and many others. I've taught courses through a Pagan seminary. I was the manager for an Ecumenical association. I'm the celebrant at a wedding this weekend on Mount Tamalpais, marrying a doctor and a biofuel researcher. It's doable, to live in community, to live with the Earth, to live in our Home as harmonious residents. It'd better be! But let me tell you, it's damn hard! It takes work. We're not gonna like everyone and they're not going to like us. But, we'd better figure it out. . .we'd better invent a new kind of community if we have to. . .*because we have to.*

One week ago today I was sitting in a Psychiatric Emergency unit with an elderly man who lives in a house I manage. He's in serious distress. He's a man of faith, but his life is fracturing and falling apart. He goes to church, but we sit in his pain and wonder, Where is his church? Where was his pastor? He didn't call them when he needed emergency help. I took him to the hospital; I took him to the psych unit. I spoke on his behalf and advocated for immediate care. I guess it's my old chaplain heart or something. . .but now I don't do it for God or the Church. I do it for him, this man, and each person who needs another human being to be present, show some basic compassion, and do something to really help. He didn't need my prayers or my bible quotes—he didn't need religion or promises or Someone up there. He needed someone who could be honest with him, to listen, to sit with him, to make some calls, to fill in some forms. In that moment, he needed *me*. I'd like to think I was helpful but I couldn't honestly do very much for this man. Yet, his smile and handshake told me I was appreciated.

I'm going to shock you right now. We need God. Yes,

we *need* God. Someone who is present, who cares, who sits with us, who has the time to get busy, who does something to help here and now, who's creative and honest and works for the good, for peace, for justice—things like that. You know. . .*God*. Right? Well, then, *Who Is that?* Right. . .You are. . .I am. No, we're not almighty and infinitely powerful and all-knowing and all that. But who needs that anyway? Maybe it's time we Play God. Join Nature and act like we're gods, because if we don't. . . . There just isn't a viable, realistic alternative.

Even the Dalai Lama, in his intriguing new book, *Beyond Religion*, grounds his call to a "secular ethics" with a very natural analogy. He says ethics *without* religion are like water. Ethics *with* religion are like tea—flavoring has been added. But, he says, *"While we can live without tea, we cannot live without water."*

Wildman Muir, sipping his watery tea from a mountain stream, by a forest campfire, was extremely impatient with all the God-talk and yet he became what I call a *natural chaplain*. He used the old language to energize for change, to get active in altering perceived realities. Muir was a master at fancy storytelling that had teeth, that caused radical change—like the invention of National Parks! Faith or no faith, everyone can enjoy the *secular sanctuaries* of the world (I've actually floated the idea of a *Moon* Wilderness Park!. . .Crazy, Nuts, Looney. . .but why not?).

Transcendent language wasn't all that important to

the man Muir. The imminently divine natural cosmos was all that mattered because it is all that IS. Nature is God, in a sense, but Nature is more. . .*Nature is actually* better *than God* because Nature (the Universe, the Cosmos) made us and everything that is (and continues to create every micro-moment), Nature gives us everything we need, we are inseparable from Nature; Nature does not demand or command or ask anything of us; Nature does not judge us or insist that we believe in it. Nature has no personality yet contains all personalities; Nature has no face but all faces. . .no need for avatars and incarnations, spirits or spiritual teachers—leave the holy books on the shelf. *Nature is fully, sufficiently enough.* Some heaven or hell or other world is completely unnecessary in a Muirian view. We come from the earth, we return to the earth. As Whitman said, we are compost. Naturally a part of the natural process, and we are no better or worse than any other lifeform. . .though we can certainly be the most destructive on the planet (when we piss in our own teacup).

Here's what Muir contemplated while walking his 1000-mile trek: "The world, we are told, was made especially for humanity--a presumption not supported by all the facts. . . ." He goes on to say, in essence, We have created our own God, no better than a cheap puppet, so no wonder we treat the "creation" so cheaply. Muir's pocket notes end with his salvation, his liberation: "Glad to leave these ecclesiastical fires and blunders, I joyfully return to the immortal truth and immortal beauty of Nature." By the way, these pages from Muir's Walk contain one of his greatest philosophical statements on preservation of the environment: He says, "The universe would be incomplete without Humanity; but it would also be incomplete without the smallest transmicroscopic creature. . . " This is the essential balance we need for a sustainable environmental ethic. We play a critical part in the Universal Play, but so does everything else.

So, you see, this is not about being anti-religious, anti-god or *anti* at all. What we're concerned with is being pro-natural, pro-common sense, pro-creativity, cooperation, collaboration; to pro-actively seek and discover solutions and make it work. Distractions or delusions of any sort are just not helpful, can be deadly and destructive and the death of our environment and our Earth--literally our demise and disappearance. Religion desperately, futilely, attempts to reach across the foggy, cloudy areas, hoping, wishing for another world, any world, better than this (I can sympathize sometimes. . .can't you?). You can almost see Muir shaking his head, scratching his bushy beard with a bewildered smile, as he reminds us, almost preaches to us: How could there ever be a more wonderful, better world! Can't we see it: *Nature is Enough! There is no super-Nature and there is no need to invent such a thing.*

In that famous story, Muir climbed a 100-foot Douglas Spruce in a Sierra windstorm, exhilarated by the high.

Have you ever felt that high? I have. For many years I've climbed a tree on Christmas Day to celebrate my birthday (not cutting a Christmas tree but climbing one!). Up there in that leafy heaven, there never fails to be a burst of energy (warms the sap in my blood!) in those balancing moments high up in the hands and arms of a living being. As Muir learned, there is always something spectacularly subtle to learn in that higher classroom!

We humans love to be amazed, mesmerized by our adventures of body or mind. . .our myths and our stories of the strange and new on the ground or up in some tree, or up in some place that feels otherworldly—we are wide-eyed with the special effects that capture our imagination. To venture into *Narnia* or the *Shire* of the Hobbits. To soar into *Pangaia* or the distant planets of *Star Trek*, *Skywalker* or the realms of dragons. Where will our imaginations take us next? Imagination is wonderful, as long as we don't lose touch and forget that we are imagining. Living in lands of make-believe would diminish the delight of Life itself.

In the Wild Gospel of Muir, it may be that what we've always thought was *spirituality was actually imagination*—pure and simple imagination. A wonderful freethinking, inventive gift of evolution. Listen closely to this mind-blowing passage from Muir's Journals:

"How infinitely superior to our physical senses are those of the mind! The spiritual eye sees not only rivers of water

but of air. . .the whole world is in motion to the center. So also Sounds. We hear only woodpeckers and squirrels and. . .streams. But imagination gives us the sweet music of tiniest insect wings, enables us to hear, all round the world, the vibration of every needle, the waving of every. . .branch. . .the sound of stars in circulation like particles in the blood. . .Imagination is usually regarded as a synonym for the unreal. Yet is true imagination healthful and real. . .Indeed, the power of imagination makes us infinite." (Journal, September, 1875)

Isn't that gorgeous? Muir has crossed over, been converted, been born again (in the words of Martin Luther King, that's when our "whole structure must be changed"). Muir was born again and again, with every sight and sound and "higher sense" of "spirituality" we can now call Mind, and Imagination. There are no limits; we are infinite. . .limitless. We ugly (maybe beautiful) bags of bacteria colonies live in a wonderful world, but one with pain and suffering and injustice, disease and death. And we'll be long gone with our science and our religion and our technology and our tantalizing distractions. . .and the earth, the cosmos, Nature will live on, forever and ever, Amen?

For now, we have the Household. What the ancients called "ecumenical"—managing the world-home. We are householders, participating in the life of the whole house. All the rooms are wirelessly inter-connected. As Muir said, you pick up one piece of it and it's hitched to everything else. And so our science; so our bio-community. As Biomimicry scientists like to say, we are only One Vote in a parliament of perhaps 100 million species. Only one vote. And, as we are learning, it is time we come to the earth, the cosmos, not simply to learn About nature, but to learn From nature. As I like to say, Nature is both Classroom and Cathedral, both Temple and Teacher.

E.O. Wilson said that humanity has a vision, a kind of spiritual craving, for an expanding future and we won't be satisfied with colonizing space. He said, "the true frontier for humanity is life on Earth"—the exploration of life on Earth leading to greater knowledge for science, art and practical affairs.

We throw around these words—Conservation. Preservation. Our mantra, "Sustainable." But, I ask again, what about Participation? What about Celebration? Sound too mystical? Not at all. Muir's sustainable enthusiasm is helpful here, and can drive on the best of science and maybe even some truly progressive "spiritual" thought and action. The entire history of human culture has been interaction with our world, participation with our world. And people have been drawn to celebrate (some would say "worship". . . though I don't think that's necessary or helpful). Maybe we don't get it, we don't understand Nature because we don't understand ourselves. We're missing something. Muir's joy, perhaps. *Pure joy in participating in the ever-delightful lessons of goodness all around us*, and—when you think of those bacteria—*within* us!

Muir's participatory wisdom echoes in the voices of

other celebrators:

Such as **Frances Wright**, an early American voice of freethought and women's rights: "The true Bible is the book of nature, the wisest teacher is the one who most plainly expounds it, the best priest our own conscience, and the most orthodox church a hall of science." (*Reason, Religion, and Morals*)

Such as **Elizabeth Cady Stanton**: "In times like this humanity rises above all college curriculums and recognizes Nature as the greatest of all teachers." (*Solitude of Self*)

We can hear Muir's voice echoing in thinkers such as **Robert Green Ingersoll**:

"One drop of water is as wonderful as all the seas; one leaf, as all the forests; and one grain of sand, as all the stars." ("The Gods")

Such as **Henry Thoreau**: "That I may dream of no heaven but that which lies about me." (Journals, March, 1856)

"It is in vain to dream of a wildness distant from ourselves. There is none such."
(Journals, August, 1856)

"I suppose that what in others is religion is in me love of nature."
(Journals, 1854?)

Such as **Theodore Roosevelt**, the President who once rolled out a blanket and camped in the snow with Muir,:

"Lying out at night under the giant sequoias had been like lying in a temple built by no hand of man, a

temple grander than any human architect could by any possibility build, and I hope for the preservation of the groves of giant trees simply because it would be a shame to our civilization to let them disappear." (speech in Sacramento, California, 1903)
And such as Muir's friend, the great naturalist, **John Burroughs**:

"Amid the decay of creeds, love of nature has high religious value. . .It has made [Nature-minded people] contented and at home wherever they are in nature—in the house not made with hands. This house is their church, and the rocks and the hills are the altars, and the creed is written in the leaves of the trees and in the flowers of the field and in the sands of the shore. [Burroughs continues] A new creed every day and new preachers, and holy days all the week through. Every walk to the woods is a religious rite, every bath in the stream is a saving [baptism]. Communion service is at all hours, and the bread and wine are from the heart and marrow of Mother Earth. There are no heretics in Nature's church; all are believers, all are communicants. The beauty of natural religion is that you have it all the time. . . .The crickets chirp it, the birds sing it, the breezes chant it, the thunder proclaims it, the streams murmur it. . . . Its incense rises from the plowed fields, it is on the morning breeze, it is in the forest breath and in the spray of the wave. . . .It is not even a faith; it is a love, an enthusiasm, a consecration to natural truth." (Accepting the Universe)

Theists and Non-Theists need to feel this poetic freedom, to engage it all, to work side by side in the present, natural world, and be charmed by Nature's seductive sacredness. We're going to have to put aside needless and unhelpful divisive, distractive debates over Super-Nature. Heaven's golden pavement no longer offers a safe ride and holy books no longer provide much more than torn and yellowed road maps for one tribe to drive over another. We need a GPS that pinpoints our place among many and includes those across borders (physical and mental). We need a Google Earth mentality that spins us around and reminds us of our journey on a very small spaceship. We need to use our telescopes and our microscopes, to get a solar view and a street view, a real perspective of where we live and a reference point for how small and inter-related we are.

We have to ask ourselves and each other: What's the alternative? Really, where else can we go with this, with what we have, with who we are? Gratefully, overall and above all, Nature is the ultimate and final organic link we have to our own humanity and this present world. I'm going to close this now and bring us back to the trailhead. . .to check the maps, take a sip of the water we are made of, and instill a little more wild wisdom from the wildman of the Sierra.

What I'm evangelizing about today is something you can put in your brain backpacks and carry into the wilds of your own mind, your own life, your own patch of the planet, your own world. . .and it's from the rugged and ragged coat pocket, under the weathered hat, of the Secular Saint, John Muir.

Where do we discover real, *sustainable secular solutions* to problems in our environment and fractures in the human community? I would suggest we remember Muir's "handy" line: "By the hands of Nature."

-Energy solutions? *By the hands of Nature.*
-Scientific, Technological, Medical solutions? *By the hands of Nature.*
-Building, Transportation, Communication solutions? *By the hands of Nature.*
-Social, neighborhood, community solutions? *By the hands of Nature.*
-Political and economic solutions? *By the hands of Nature.*
-Personal, psychological solutions? *By the hands of Nature.*
And the mind, the imagination, the poetry, the pure delight. . .of Nature.

I'd like to conclude with a kind of Benediction from our Secular Saint, drawn from his journals:

"We little know how much wildness there is in us."
"GO now and then for fresh life. . . just as divers hold their breath and come to the surface to breathe. . . Go whether or not you have faith. . . Go to the snowflowers in winter, Go to the sunflowers in summer. . . Go up and away for Life!"
"GO, free as the wind, living as true to Nature. . .as the sequoias and the pines."

"May New Beauty meet you at every step in all your

wanderings."
2012

11

How Green is God?

In the years since "renouncing" my ordination, I rarely get invited to speak in a Presbyterian Church. The pastor of one local church in California knew me well, and her congregation included some of my former seminary professors as well as people who knew my work as a chaplain and shelter director. Asked to give the Sunday sermon, I knew my words would stretch some of them, but they couldn't have been too offended since they invited me back. My sermon title was "God is Green" and the scripture texts were "Nature and selections from the Letter of James."

A few years ago I lived on an island in my home state of Washington (now I consider myself a hybrid *Washingfornian*). On the island I lived in a small one-room cabin and worked on an organic farm, planting, pulling tons of weeds, harvesting, and clearing trails through the thick, dripping, mossy-green forest. One afternoon, while deep in the woods, I poked my right eye tossing vines and sticks into the brush. Nursing my blurry eye back at the cabin, I heard a swooshing sound and looked up. On a low alder branch sat one of my near neighbors: the barred owl. I walked near the tree as she stared down. Then I noticed she had one eye closed (I'm not making this up)—her *right eye* was closed. I smiled at her winged sympathy, and gave a bow to my neighbor on her bough. My sight was impaired but I had a moment of vision, of insight into what could be called the Greenness of God.

There is a great deal of talk these days about *Being Green*. A Green Revolution. Green is the New Cool. A kind of Religion, isn't it? Green evangelists telling us where to shop, what to buy, what to eat, what to drive, what to conserve, what not to throw away—as Kermit the Frog used to say: It's not easy being Green!

Green is planted deep in our language: green with envy; green behind the ears; greenback; greensleeves; Green Day; village green; putting green; green belt; Green Beret; green around the gills; green horn; greenhouse; greengrocer; green card; greenskeeper; green room; greenwood; green light; green tea. . .

We are clearly verdant, virescent beings—always becoming green and growing greener.

Did you read the headline in yesterday's *San Francisco Chronicle*? "Birds Damaged 45 Planes at SFO." This shows you how my mind works: I immediately turned it around—*45 Planes Kill Birds at SFO!*

I guess I'm beginning to think Green, naturally. I find I have more of a feeling for, a connection with, the Pagan view of the earth: *pagan* just means country-folk (outsiders who live outside close to the ground; it's like the old word, *heathen*—meaning people of the heath and heather, or that great word *heretic*: one who chooses another—green?—path). Pagan, heathen, heretic—these outsiders have no fear of the dirt; they aren't afraid of becoming impure or stained by the natural environment. They see Life in the earth, the Earth is Alive, and all living things are animated— they are *anima*--there is living soul or spirit or breath within it all.

Pagans get really excited about Green. Pagans, Wiccans and a lot of indigenous tribal people are members of the original Green Religion—Nature Religion—Nature as Religion, or at least some kind of directly experienced spirituality.
Theologians (that is, those who make good guesses about things they really don't know anything about) refer to this ancient philosophy of earthiness as either animism or Pantheism—all is imbued with life, every particle and proton teeming with electricity and aliveness—a relationship is possible with the earth, with nature, the Universe. . .or call it God. . .it doesn't matter. The relationship is everything—and it is a relationship with Everything, as a part of every last thing. Creator and creation are one.

The great naturalist John Burroughs said that we get into great trouble when we identify God with Nature. But, Burroughs says. . .What trouble we get into when we refuse to identify the two! God and Nature are the same thing, in Burroughs 'mind. God is Nature and Nature is God. Seems natural doesn't it? Maybe not. So either God is literally Green (and brown, red, yellow, white, blue—*earth tones*) or out there, as the old song says, somewhere beyond the sea, or beyond the sky.

Burroughs put it this way:
"We go away from home [the earth, the known universe] searching for the gods [the spiritual]—gods that we carry with us always." What does that mean? We search for the backpack and behold, it's been on our back the whole time. We have been hoodwinked into thinking that there are two universes: one physical and one spiritual—one natural and one super-natural. The gospel of Burroughs, and Muir and many other scientific-naturalists calls us to return to our roots, literally, our dark brown and green roots. In this view and practice, spirituality is simply our life—nothing more, nothing less.

What's the alternative?. . *James.*

So, what was James' problem? He didn't like green! He wasn't green, didn't care to even notice the green. He was too busy doing what a lot of religious people do: keeping his eye on the sky (particularly the cloudy, stormy, gray, judgment-looking sky) and hoping for a quick trip to the very un-green wilderness above. Heaven, as you know, is a very un-Green place! Everything's gold and pearls and, by god, there's no recycling!!

James presents us with the old theology of separation:

the earth and humanity is— worldly, fleshly, dirty, sinful, from below; the good and divine is—heavenly, unstained, pure, from above. . .

Simple. And gravely simplistic.

The writer of the Book of James lost what Emerson called "the love of Beauty." Sadly, James has lost a deep and energizing, creative and positive sense of beauty —intrinsic beauty. John Muir said that Beauty is the best synonym for the divine. God equals Beauty in the way Nature equals God.

James preaches the *Theology of Separation* (human from divine; natural from super-natural; below from above). And the question must be asked: *Is this a helpful or healthy theology, for then or now?*

It is a Theology of UP-looking, that tramples the plants and animals and fellow humans while gazing up into the cloud mansions looking for another world of purity and glory—it's always about glory; always for the "pure" and "holy" ones: the saints. . .Us, and certainly not Them or Their World.

This is the *Theology of all Fanatics and Fundamentalists*. I know, I used to be one. In my opinion, this dim and dim-witted theology is not only unhelpful but ultimately destructive to everything in its path. It is *Religion of the Battleground*, where everything is a constant battle for the Right and the Righteous. It is about division, sectarianism and faith-based fear as well as fear-based faith.

But what if Burroughs is right—what if there is no separation? What if there is only Nature? Or if you prefer, what if there is only God? What about the natural world? Does this transform our out-looking and up-looking into an in-looking and a down-looking? Or simply a wider, more inclusive, more balanced, more curious, inquisitive, delighted looking?

And what if John Muir was on the right trail: he challenged us to go further into Nature's Temples, our parks and open spaces and even our gardens and backyards and our own inseparable nature, because there—which is really here—is the only place to find anything that could be called "divine." In Muir's perspective, why do we keep filling libraries with holy books and filling the earth with holy houses of worship all cut, carved and constructed from the living temples, the living churches of Nature? We live in the Sanctuary and don't even know it. And this sanctuary is open 24/7, has no doors or stained glass or altars because it is all one great green altar. In fact, it has no altar either, because there is no more sacrifice or appeasing to be done.

The green church needs no clergy or creed or confession. This sanctuary is green, leafy, wild, alive through and through, it is the abode of eagles and whales, of orangutans and owls, of wolves and bears and lions, of snails and slugs and spiders and bugs—all calling us into the greenness because We are Green, God is Green, and we don't even seem to care.

Why? Why don't we care? Because so much religion and faith is *Jamesian*. Martin Luther wanted to rip the Letter of James right out of the Bible. His reason was its emphasis on Works rather than Faith. My reason would be its emphasis on Faith rather than Reason, on the Super-natural over the Natural, its insistence on being Gray and not Green (by the way, I like the color gray and I like storm clouds too—but that's not my point either. . .yet, maybe it is!).

There are some important lessons in James. The instructions about caring for widows and orphans are good reminders (though we already know it's the right thing to do, don't we?). Urging the Christian community to care for poorer Christians is admirable (though we could wish compassion might extend to some of the outsiders—maybe a Pagan or two). And "love your neighbor as yourself" isn't a bad ethic. No, don't tear James out of the scriptures. *Just bring a green marking pen when you read it.* On the other hand, it might make great mulch for the garden vegetables—but don't quote me on that.

One of the greatest orators of the 19th Century, Robert Ingersoll (whose middle name was, seriously, *Green*—Robert *Green* Ingersoll) once said that the American Founders learned from Nature and used what they learned from the natural world to become as great as the land. Jefferson, Paine, Adams, Washington, Madison. . .they learned from Nature and became *as great as the land*. When people learn from the land, their land, Nature, they share in the greatness, the beauty, the divinity (?) of the only home we know. This seems noble; this seems revolutionary and the stuff of reformation; this seems "faithful"; and it sounds "sustainable"—even "organic." Are we as great as our land?

The writer of James forgot, or maybe he never learned, to love the dirt, to go skinny dipping in a river, to walk in a forest or climb a mountain, to make love or write a poem—to get *stained* by the World. He forgot to be like the farmer waiting for the precious crop from the earth, not a promise from the sky. He forgot, but we don't have to.

We need the Green. My mother always raised her eyebrows when I came in from playing and my pants were covered with grass-stains and my shirt was sticky with sap from climbing the pines, firs and cedars, or crawling around through the laurel. Bless you mom, but my mother the Earth washes in other ways. The chlorophyll and the tree sap are as clean as my blood and brain.

It's time for us to let go of our weary worldly worries. Why don't we wash off all these obsessions about dirt and doubt and disbelief? Let's try to practice something healthier by getting a lasting scrub, a fresher clean, by getting more grounded, by getting immersed, baptized even, in the goodness and gritty green all around us.

This is our life. There is no other world. Green is naturally God or God is naturally green. And maybe one day, this will be exactly what we mean by "Faith."

2009

12

Green Village

Written when I was the emergency winter shelter director for Marin County, just north of San Francisco, this continues the green-theme, grounded in the human need for shelter.

At a shelter the other night one of our most active volunteers said to me, "If the church, if I, could just help one of these guys get off the street, I'd be happy." I assured him that helping one would make a difference—and that assisting one, just one, is a respectable, practical and sensible beginning.

All throughout this shelter season (as I tried hard to direct this un-directable experiment) I have seen staff, volunteers and our guests themselves interacting with others in caring and positive ways. "How's John doing today?"; "Will Millie be coming back soon?"; "Jenny isn't looking well. She needs to see a nurse." Questions and comments that reflect the kind of relational caring this program is based upon.

Now, congregations are struggling with how to help people, one by one, before and after the shelter closes. In a few short weeks hundreds of volunteers from dozens of congregations will be saying "Goodbye" to our guests. It's always hard when you're a host to say goodbye to guests you have grown to like and respect. And, yes, it can be a relief as well. That's honest. It's time for a change. But this time, this season, with this shelter, something seems different. People have genuinely connected to each other, one by one. "Homeless People" and "The Religious" now have names, faces, lives to share. Out of this connection, many in congregations are meeting to ask the hard questions and make difficult decisions: "How can we help *these* people, people we know, and help them *now*?" "I feel bad that I can only help one person or that my congregation can do so little." "What if we can only find one of our friends a job, or a room, or give them a ride, or take them out to lunch?" All legitimate, heartfelt and reasonable questions and concerns.

One way we are addressing our struggles is to openly discuss specific people and how more than one congregation can work side by side with another to continue the relationships. At one meeting a pastor said her church was hoping to help one of the staff. Then two other congregations said they were concerned about the same person. The three of them are now discussing a collaborative response. We have heard from Adopt-a-Family and the Open Table program about what might work for us. And we are picking up ideas from staff and guests as well. One person mentioned opening a camping area for legal, permitted camping (and safe, legal parking for "metal homes").

Which leads to the next discussion.

I had a very lively conversation with one staff-member, Albert, and several of our guys in the shelter last evening. We were tossing around a wild and revolutionary idea that we named "Green Village." It reflects how "out of the boxes" (homes and minds) we have to venture to create something better, something that works, for housing and human community. This is a giant step away from the unsightly, unsafe and unsanitary "tent city" or "shantytown" messes in some areas. "Green Village" would be a circle of tipis (cheap, portable, sturdy, time-tested dwellings) on public or private land, pleasing to the eye and respectful of the land, managed by some of our staff, with solar-power, low water use, compost toilets and an organic garden. A central meeting space, around a common fire circle, would create an open, inclusive "spiritual" space for meetings, services and events. A model "sustainable" village, somewhat based on ancient tribal communities.

The old and outdated term "homeless" would just dissolve into the ground, dissipate into thin air. Albert feels that people would come from everywhere just to see the village and learn from the simplicity of people living in an earth-friendly community. Social workers, medical professionals, job counselors, chaplains and the sheriff would make regular visits to support and encourage the clean, sober and safe environment. "Green Village," with its small footprint, would be the best of Marin County, at the forefront of both the movement for creative housing solutions and environmental sensitivity (featured no doubt in *Sunset Magazine* and given international attention!). . .and provide housing, work and supportive community for many who cannot sustain the standard of lifestyle required to "fit in" to Marin. Businesses like George Lucas' Industrial Light and Magic and Autodesk, successful musicians and artists, investors, congregations and environmental organizations would want to buy into this model. It is a win-win model that benefits everyone.

By the way, if this looks like just another new-agey ripoff of Native American culture, consider that we have been sheltering Native people from various tribes both last season and this season (and many of our guests live "in the elements," close to the earth, day and night). "Green Village" is a natural, respectful honoring of what we have lost by forcing indigenous peoples and ourselves into an artificial, unneighborly *Culture of Boxes* where the only "central fire" is the glowing television or computer screen in each locked box. Besides, the irony should not be lost either: when we are struck by an earth-shaker similar to Haiti or Chile (and we will be), and our boxes crumble to little pieces, we will need shelter, and the only shelter left may be "Green Village" whose inhabitants will be our hosts, and we will be *their* guests.

Is this completely crazy? A bizarre dream? Probably not. Is it crazier than playing the "housing element" numbers game with city after city, or pumping millions into new shelters and programs for "the homeless?" Is it more bizarre than arresting people for sleeping outside or criminalizing people without houses? Wouldn't this take years to develop and huge amounts of cash? I don't think so.

The County, in partnership with a landowner, congregations and environmentalists should deem the housing crisis a Present Emergency, immediately opening some land for the project (always an obstacle, but this isn't a tent city or a housing development). Community partnerships, with the Marin Community Foundation, could assist with the purchase of materials including the tipis (several thousand dollars apiece). Architects, conservationists, sustainable farming folks and Village residents could help develop the layout, build the foundations and set up the tipis, the compost toilets, common kitchen areas, etc. Congregations, schools, clubs, agencies and families could "sponsor" a tipi, helping furnish each dwelling and monitoring upkeep (individuals and families could enjoy regular visits to stay connected to "Village Life"). For another working example of this type of community, see Portland, Oregon's Dignity Village.

How many of our sheltering hosts and supporters would get excited about this innovative concept? How many would want to be directly involved in a project like "Green Village?" See why we have to be careful when we listen to those "on the outside," who think outside the boxes because they live outside them?! In the immediacy of the next few weeks we may not be able to open a "Green Village" —we may not think this is do-able right now, or at all, but what is the alternative? Really, what is left? The same old sheltering and housing approaches, that try to make people live the way "civilized" people live—get a good income, a big house, a car and pay your taxes on your pretty boxes. Think what it would be like to have people living "the old way," as most of our ancestors lived, close to the earth, the ground, in circles around a central fire, when true community meant that no neighbor was excluded, each was known by each and everyone made a valuable contribution, each had a vital part. Could "Green Village" lead the way forward, with a step back to what life was meant to be?

Maybe we can help one person now. Maybe two or three congregations can be companions for one or two of our guests. Maybe connecting a person to a room or a job is all we have the time for. Perhaps some of us can still eat lunch at the St. Vinnie's free dining room and mingle again with people as their guests, in their community, on their "unholy" ground. This makes a huge difference in that person's life, and ours. And together, would it be too wild to say that we can make the "Green Village" a reality as we are reaching out a helping hand to each individual, one by one, life by life?

2010

13

A Touch of Death

*"The fear of death is the beginning of philosophy,
and the final cause of religion."*
~Will Durant, The Story of Philosophy

The touch of his face felt as waxy as the look of his skin. There was something intensely unreal to the look, the touch, yet at the same instant it was the most real I could ever see, could ever touch. I had touched death before, another's, my own. This time the waxy look and feel of it melted onto me a little more. Death had a face, a young face, and it was as if my own life mask was beginning to heat and drip, re-molding into something I could not put my hand on yet. Because I knew my touch was not my own alone, this touch held a deeper significance than any I could remember. A few miles away sat a man, a father, who could not touch his dead son and who never would.

The night before, I had listened to the father whisper his grief to me, eyes as wide and captured in that dark, chilled space as a caged leopard. And so he felt; so in some sense he was. He blew a curling cloud of smoke down and away like his voice, making visible the words of his story that made my eyes water along with the drifting smoke. He had made some unwise choices, been stupid and selfish. Now he was encaged in a cold, dark, loud and smoky jail cell. So near his family, so far. Torn apart but forced to "keep it together" he chose to speak to someone and that someone was me. All I could do was show up, be there, hear him—to be what I was, a human being and a chaplain. I was a chaplain, his chaplain, for that night at least, the night he was living while his son lay dead. His son had died suddenly the day before. A collect call home from the phone in the cell confirmed it. He could do nothing. Steel and cement contained him with emotions no parent should ever feel or feel contained with. The other men in his cell laughed, smoked, played cards on the steel tables, stared at some meaningless television show, lay on bunks reading or snoring. This man, crouching inches from my face, whispered his pain with the cold and empty breath of helplessness. I listened, ear next to the dusty bars, and could only listen though the listening was difficult surrounded by slamming doors and flushing toilets, shouts and cursing, arguments and blaring boxes of distracting entertainment.

The father could not be distracted. He was publicly grieving in silence, in an inner cell of guarded privacy. Our private conversation of death went unnoticed surrounded by living, breathing, moving cells locked into their own hidden security. There was something freeing in listening to this one voice among many, the voice of the unfree.

Our quiet moments enveloped in noise, straining to hear, holding each other's eyes, led into a simple request. Would I be willing to go to his house where his family was holding a wake, a vigil, by the body of his son? Would I go and be his eyes, his fingers, his grief embodied, to touch his son for him? Someone shouted for a deputy, another, for a pack of smokes. All I could hear, all I could feel and think about, was one quiet, simple question. I nodded, assuring him I would honor his request; he gripped my hand, we sighed and composed ourselves to face others. But there was only one face, his. The next face I would look into would not look back.

I have no memory of any other conversations with any others that night, no other words or faces, the touch of no other hands, the look of no other eyes but the father's. I did what I always did, what no one in there could do that night or for many nights: I walked out the doors. Door after heavy door.   Steel gates sliding and slamming. Before me, behind me. Pushing open the last glass door I emerged into the night, the real night, with fresh, enlivening air, sounds of cars and dogs barking, stars overhead. As I crossed the parking lot I shuddered with the almost sickening sense that I had warped across worlds. With some trembling I unlocked another door, one I could control, and sat behind the wheel of my truck. I had to just sit for a long minute, to touch my own face, my own feelings.

And I drove away from the bright lights spotlighting that dark place like a stage, wondering if all the passing people really felt safer, protected from the men and women I had just sat with, spoke with and touched. My winding drive home was question mark after question mark. I locked myself into my dark cell of wood—not steel—and with the usual half-sleep, walked along corridors of half-dreams all night.

The door was open. The house was full of family and friends. Incense filled the air along with puffs of pot. The color-coated autumn day was clear but oddly warm. A woman walked up to touch my hand and welcome me. "He called and said you would come." A child ran by, another sat and stared across the room. A couple sat close, touching hands, whispering softly as they leaned temple to temple. Several guys stood on the porch nursing beers. The couch was set up like a bed, not a casket or a grave; it was a place of rest, a memorial with the memorialized present, silent. Photos, candles, pieces of his life around him, on him. I smiled and nodded. These were not a people afraid of death, to look at it, have it among them, give it a central seat in the room.

At that moment no one stood or knelt by him, by the son. I slowly moved to his side. I crouched low and close as I had done with his dad. The young man had something of a look of peace. His skin was slightly pale though the brown of his ancestry almost glowed. There may have been music playing; I have no memory. Some may have glanced to watch the stranger kneeling by the body. I didn't see or hear. I leaned close to sense the person, the life lying there, but leaned closer to the dead, to the open cell of death. And I placed my palm on his forehead, closed my eyes but couldn't keep them closed. I drew a deep, calm breath and felt minutes blow passed. I was praying without words or even prayer. I was touching what was once conscious life conscious of my hand, that it was more than my hand. *I was a father touching with a father's hand*—all fathers' hands. I felt the touch of my own father's big, squeezing hand as he said goodbye and faded behind me as I closed a final door. I felt for an instant the fragile fingers of my baby daughter on the day of her birth.

None of this conscious. There was nothing there, no one. Not a thought, a prayer or even a tangible god. I placed my hand on death with respect, with respect for death, and for life, the son's, the father's, my own. I smelled the incense that could never incinerate separation, finality--only remind of it, welcome its swirling, ascending freedom. Nothing was incarcerated here. Yet, death was incarnate. I drew a long breath and bowed, a grateful breath of free air freely taken. I was the father. I was the father present, touching, breathing, breathing free, who was releasing, liberating the son. I was nothing more, no one more than one man serving another man by a simple act of touch.

When I last saw the father he was still inside. Inside the same cell, the same feelings. He firmly grasped my hand and nodded at my words. His face looked like wax, ready to burn, to melt. He was now listening to me with the same attentiveness that possessed me kneeling by his son. He grasped every word of my description, of his son, the gathered family, the life I felt there. Maybe he felt he had now said the beginning of his goodbyes, that he was freer to grieve and go on. I don't really know. How can anyone know those thoughts, those feelings? His nod was a bow, a thanks without words when there could be no words.

I cannot recall anything we said or if it was a minute or an hour. I know we touched. I know our eyes were wet, blurred. I know I felt privileged in a way I have rarely felt. I would like to think he caught just a scent of that incense as I left, in the wake of freedom, through an open door to the vigil of whispered wishes.

2006

14

Wonder and Wildness

> *". . .[Scientific passion]. . .is summed up in that*
> *childlike, but infinitely complex word, wonder. . .*
> *Wonder. . .goes through various stages, evolving*
> *both with age and with knowledge, but retaining*
> *an irreducible fire and spontaneity."*
> ~Richard Holmes, The Age of Wonder

We moved to Western North Carolina in 2016, yet the
images and sensations described in this essay stick to my
mind like a burr on a pant-leg

I started writing a little book, calling it "Divorcing the Divine: The Good and the Great Beyond God." Catchy title. I thought of weaving "lessons" from my experiences of failed marriage into some understanding of failed faith. I only got as far as comparing "irreconcilable differences" and emotional stress before realizing this endeavor was not going to be much fun and even less enlightening, at least at this point in time.

One analogy from this "failed book" lingered because it has to do with fingers and touch, wetness and wildness. No, it's not what you're thinking. But it is the story of my enjoyment touching beetles and bees, un-nameable bugs and nonchalant newts, even spiders and snakes.

I currently live near the San Francisco Bay which I can see a sliver of across the pastureland, passed the eucalyptus and ponds beyond. The ponds (I like to call them "lakes") are part of the sanitary district's water treatment plant that I often refer to as "the sewer factory" which of course it is not. When I walk on the gravelly and grassy pathways around these ponds and saunter further along the muddy rivulets and salty marshlands I frequently see a colorful variety of birds. Egrets, ducks, clapper rails, cormorants, green herons, owls and other residents can be seen and heard in the company of Canada geese and huge white pelicans gliding over solitary Great Blue herons in their balanced, meditative poses.

Keep in mind, these are "sanitary ponds" with "reclaimed water." Now and then we even spy a playful pair of river otters. It all seems quite wild, in a suburban kind of way. Along these walks, especially on the levees crisscrossing the marshlands, I often spot a rippled brown stick across the path ahead that causes me to slow and proceed on full alert. More often than not this "stick" transforms into a snake. Though we have rattlesnakes in the area, this particular micro-climate eco-system generates large numbers of mice, duck eggs and gophers, hence a most ideal habitat for the gopher snake. While these slithering, scaly creatures can get fairly large, most are only a few feet long, a couple of inches around and harmless to anyone who isn't tiny, furry, four-legged or on the half-shell.

What I like to do, when I haven't frightened the snake away, is to stop, speak softly (out of habit) and slowly bend down for a closer look. I'm fascinated by the intensity of these silent predators, fully aware that I'm no doubt interrupting their shopping-hunt for food. If I'm close enough, and the creature seems distracted, I lean down and softly … slowly … gently … *touch*. Only once has one turned toward me and (I'm sure I heard this) hissed. The best moments are when the snake hasn't rushed off and I can slowly stand erect and step away to continue on. Then I can at least imagine that I haven't caused much disturbance or re-inforced his/her fearful, defensive instinct against yet another threatening human.

Yet, at the same moment, I'm also aware this animal is indeed threatened and may not be alive to be seen another day, on another walk. Parts of these levee trails are regularly mowed or weed-whacked and a fairly steady stream of walkers (too many with canines, in my opinion) as well as runners and bikers come along. It's possible that most gopher snakes end up as food for the very creatures who are their main competitors in the hunt for food: the raptors. This is prime hawk country, and owls nest in these parts too. So it's just as likely I won't see any one particular snake again unless it can avoid all the dangers of being a fairly defenseless, slow-slithering ground-dweller.

When it comes to trail encounters with newts and bees and slugs and just about anything that won't fang my finger, *I'm a toucher*—I sense there is a deep-set need to make contact, if only for a brushing moment. Yes, I understand that the oils and bacterias on the human skin can cause harm to some creatures. I'm aware and try to be careful. I acknowledge this is my need, my curiosity at play here, and maybe it's more play than I admit, but I don't think so. I think it is the contact and even a fleeting sense of *relation* and maybe *inter-dependence*. A vestige of my "spirituality"? Exactly. But this is so much better, and fulfilling and, I would say without hesitation, more wise and respectful and present, with so much more potential for learning just about anything and everything I have to learn. That's saying a lot, I know. I know.

And, so, you may be thinking, what's all this have to do with anything resembling "spirituality" and wonder and such? If you have to ask …

Identifying and, I guess in some sense calling for, a conclusion to this thing we've always referred to as *spirituality*, is asking for a divorce because there is no relationship remaining. There is no life left, no health, no energy, no delight. There is no real connection, no electric touch, no commitment, no will to love and learn and journey on together. Honesty calls for an admission: *the wonder is gone.*

The same for faith, god, religion and any form of supernatural hokum and poke-us. The otherworldly realm of "spirituality" offers, when you bend right down and touch it, nothing—no wonder, no joy, no hope, no actual *touch* at all. For many of us, it leaves one disappointed, feeling jilted, depressed. But then, with patience on the path, step by step, comes the good part—liberation, moving on, living onward.

Recovering wonder can be like recovering sanity and stability after the trauma of addiction or a failure or loss of any kind.

In my first Philosophy text in college, *The Story of Philosophy*, Will Durant introduced us to the "love of wisdom" by introducing us to the troubling dichotomies of our time, badly in need of that wisdom. The radical faults, fractures and divorces between people and worldviews were due in part to the observation that, "Human knowledge [has] become too great for the human mind." Even as he writes in the mid-twentieth century, Durant reasons we are overloaded (sound familiar?), splintering into fields of specialization. He says, "The specialist [put] on blinders in order to shut out from his vision all the world but one little spot, to which he glued his nose. Perspective was lost." Then the gap between knowledge and what we do with that knowledge grew wider. "In the midst of unprecedented learning, popular ignorance flourished, and chose its exemplars to rule the great cities of the world; in the midst of sciences endowed and enthroned as never before, new religions were born every day, and old superstitions recaptured the ground they had lost. The common person found themselves forced to choose between a scientific priesthood mumbling unintelligible pessimism, and a theological priesthood mumbling incredible hopes."

Amazingly well said. I haven't yet found myself in complete agreement with the historian, that the last century was at this extreme of bifurcation, rent asunder by either pessimism or un-believable hope; on the other hand ... I suppose it can't be denied that we were cut apart (by wars, politics, culture, race, gender, religion, etc), and the gulf has only widened in our minds and thereby the corporate schizophrenia has permeated our communities, our nations, our world. Polarization is the new norm (note: I wrote this almost ten years ago). And how "new" is that? He's right though, "priesthoods" claim their authority and vie for our allegiance. We'd better be thinking or the "popular ignorance" will continue to flourish and infect. Philosophy can't be the only answer; a rigorous practice of pragmatic wisdom can't be the only solution. Or? Can you name another? Spirituality? Really? Should we choose the old superstitions and allow them to "recapture the ground they had lost"? Sad to say, we tend toward escapes, dodges, avoidance, denial and distraction. Drugs or the supernatural? Pick your poison.

All those years ago, reading Durant alongside my Bible, yellow highlighted and worn with use, as I was emerging from my saturated evangelical worldview/ heavenview, I was beginning to pay attention to the mumblings from all sides, and wonder: can we think and reason our way through and out, out of the caves of ignorance (echoes of Plato), beyond the gods we have known? And I wonder still. We have to, don't you think? Don't we think? How delightful to participate in the voyages, the expeditions, the adventures of discovery available on every saunter into the natural world! How incredibly enlivening to retain that "irreducible fire and spontaneity"!

The disturbing point is, the voice of reason is now going to be heard on a regular basis—the bells of Freethought are ringing from someplace other than crosscrowned towers—and the more those voices and those bells are heard, the more religious and spiritual claims to divine authority are going to be challenged and dragged into what John Burroughs called "the light of day." It's not always pretty or fun, only essential, and so freeing.

It's time—it's always time—to touch the wildness, of Nature, of our own nature, of what it means to be a wondering, wonder-full human being. I will continue to touch because I would rather touch and feel more human, more alive, when I touch the snake and the bee, the newt and the spider (particularly the tiny jumping variety), as well as another fellow homo sapiens. Each and all mean more than an imagined heaven above and beyond where the disconnect—the divorce—is enthroned for eternity. Here, and gladly here, we are in the greatest garden of eden imaginable (where snakes are not feared, and can be touched), fruited and fed, shaded and sheltered by the ever-growing, everevolving tree of knowledge and life. And it is a forest of trees. It is good, isn't it? Wild, wonderful, always evolving, endlessly creating and very good.

2013

15

Living Bridge

"I have never tried to clothe myself in the delusive garments of a superstitious age. I have never pinned my faith to a man-made God, however venerable. I have opened my mind to the open air of the universe, to things as they are."
~ John Burroughs, Accepting the Universe

Recently I stepped carefully across a fallen tree spanning a cold, forest stream, aware that there was both steady and streaming life below my feet, as well as towering over my head in the silent redwood cathedral. I stopped in the middle to settle into the unsettledness of being suspended, held in a dangerously wonderful moment. In these times, when I used to think of other worlds and bow to an unseen Presence above or behind Nature, I now find a new practice, a new way of seeing, a new balance. In some sense I have "crossed over" a living bridge identified by a small number of a new breed of "spiritual teacher," including the wise and balancing thinker, John Burroughs (1837-1921).

It was a delight to discover two major streams of

Burroughs' thought. He was first and foremost a naturalist, a scientific adventurer who was an enthusiastic lover of the natural world. He was, secondly and significantly, a spiritual (poetic and philosophical) adventurer who redefined spirituality, religion, faith and God for a more reasonable, enlightened world. Here, I primarily reflect on Burroughs' face in the swirling confluence of streams—his potent and potential contribution to a wider understanding of faith and reason, of science and religion, of Nature itself.

One of my favorite passages in the corpus of JB literature, found in my 1908 printing of *Leaf and Tendril*, is in the chapter, "The Art of Seeing Things." In his playfully profound way, Burroughs offers these wise observations:

"The book of nature is like a page written over or printed upon with different-sized characters and in many different languages, interlined and cross-lined, and with a great variety of marginal notes and references ... . We all read the large type more or less appreciatively, but only the students and lovers of nature read the fine lines and the footnotes."

A few paragraphs later he describes his June walk and discovery of wild bees. He sees tiny mounds of earth he had never seen before. In his expansive curiosity he stops, stoops and spies the life at his feet, saying to himself, "Here is some fine print that I have overlooked." And, the keen observer says, "So I set to work to try to read it; I waited for a sign of life." A bit later he muses, "One seldom takes a walk without encountering some of this fine print on nature's page."

In the many years I served as a chaplain on the wild edges of my community, among marginalized folk in dark jails and on dirty streets, I often stopped to pay better attention, to kneel and squint to read volumes of fine print and footnotes in the margins of our neighborhoods. Though I didn't know John Burroughs at that time, his mindful principles were active. From the most unexpected places, from the most hidden human beings, I heard because I listened, and I saw because I used my eyes to see. I taught classes in World Faiths, leading discussions on Sacred Scriptures and traditions; I presided at countless memorials and other "celebrations of life." I sat and walked, laughed and cried with the outsiders, until the castaway community in the urban wilderness became my own.

Decades of "presence ministry" with invisible outcasts, from community and church, surprised me with a renewed sense of inter-connection; I felt related to other human beings who struggled to find a balance or a place to stand, "a place to belong" as one home-seeking man put it. And along the way it was the grittiness and messiness of life, the most troubling questions of suffering friends, and the oddly wonderful beauty embedded there, that led me to feel a deep discomfort with my faith and the "holy books" we cut and carve from living things. The distractions of religion simply became irrelevant to me, to my work. I began to see the wild bees—what I had never seen before.

On my daily paths and trails, year after year, what was once "sacred" dissolved, evaporated into living with others in a radically secular world. It simply became natural to be a companion alongside fellow creatures while allowing them to be my teachers, my trailguides, helping me to see better, to appreciate more, to keep crossing over to the present (the secular), with a "sacred" (inter-related) grounding in the here and now. Along the twisted pathway, all heavy books of belief were removed from my pack, each un-grounded, un-natural spirituality was let go and dropped, when I gained a Burroughs'-eye-view of things.

As readers of Burroughs and students of Nature's Book ("Nature's Bible" for John Muir), we may find some relief in that he felt no need to reach deep into his religious childhood to state what many would say is obvious: this Book of Nature is written by God and holds divine lessons. He saw no obvious conclusion on that; he felt no need to follow that ancient riverbed; his views had changed, he had crossed over, to another way of understanding, a fresh way of seeing. He understood the super-natural interpretations of the world (like Muir he was steeped and stewed in them), but he came to see that these were inadequate; *Nature needs no super*, no artificial additives or un-natural ingredients. In crossing over (actually wading into) the stream of life, he was, in my opinion, crossing back from the otherworldly to the this-worldly, from the sacred to the secular. And, in the process, in the fine balance, Burroughs was offering us a delicate sprig of green, a sip of clear water, a living gift that helps us step in the direction of a sacred-secular unity. He presents us with perhaps our new *secular scripture*. I imagine millions ready to turn those leafy pages.

John Burroughs makes it a bit easier to read. With aid of microscope, telescope, and that amazing invention of evolution, the eye, JB invites us to participate in "Accepting the Universe" (his pioneering 1920 book) seeking the "Signs and Seasons" (a 1904 piece) to make a decisive step into "The Light of Day" (his seminal work from 1900). In *The Light of Day*, what we might call a "secular sermon," he reveals the foundation of the bridge he is building:

"To find the divine and the helpful in the mean and familiar, to find religion without the aid of any supernatural machinery, to see the spiritual, the eternal life in and through the life that now is—in short, to see the rude, prosy earth as a star in the heavens, like the rest, is indeed the lesson of all others the hardest to learn."

Many of us who have left the religious side of the stream welcome the lesson even as we share Burroughs' critiques of any spirituality past or present. We still have loved and respected ones who choose to hold onto the far bank, to their own trees of "Truth." We want to be in relationship with the believers in their houses of faith while being content with moving on up or down the open, inviting trails in the immense, roofless cathedral of the cosmos. Any honest theist or atheist could say an "Amen!" to these words from our natural chaplain:

"Every [person] builds or tries to build a house of truth of some sort, to shelter [them] from the great void, but how foolish to expect us all to build alike or go to the same quarry for our material; or that our house could serve for our children for all coming time. How long it will serve depends upon how large, how well, how conveniently it is built."

With this in mind, we might value Burroughs as a constructive, progressive, "ecumenical" (world-house managing) minister, in the best sense of these words.

Burroughs, the intrepid intellectual explorer, won't let us rest or settle for long in the middle of any stream or thought. His agitating impatience really moves us to an almost Buddhist acceptance of impermanence. Yet, he offers more. He offers "the faith of a naturalist" (*Accepting the Universe*) that takes some of the most highly charged words back from the super-naturalists, as in this beloved passage:

"Amid the decay of creeds, love of nature has high religious value. . .[a lover of nature] is at home wherever they are in nature. . . . this house is their church. . .every walk to the woods is a religious rite. . . . Communion service is at all hours. . . . There are no heretics in Nature's church. . . . it is not even a faith; it is a love, an enthusi-

asm, a consecration to natural truth."

As a former minister, who once held tightly to the tangled theologies on one side of the stream, I am deeply grateful for the re-definitions as well as the fearless discarding of distracting words and opinions that kept me from a free crossing. It can be unnerving as well as wildly exhilarating to leave the hopes and dreams of other worlds, other realities, to come back down to the rich, brown earth. Life can be extremely muddy and uncertain along the banks and shorelines, the edges, the margins and the borderlands that divide. But what a liberation to leap onto the slippery but solid ground of the "holy land" that is our eternal, virescent home! And how good it is when people on different sides bring their diversity to the precarious center, respectfully building on creative alternatives in a spirit of cooperation, collaboration and community, daring new forms of communication. What a healthier, more sustainable environment is possible when we simply choose to "step out on a limb" to discover common roots!

The introduction to my little book, *Meditations of John Burroughs: Nature is Home* (2007), opens with a reference to JB's birth in the mountains of New York in 1837 and his death on a train returning from California in 1921. For me, these are the bookends to a bountiful life, East and West, symbolic of "a man who spanned distances in life and in death." He remains a bridge, a bridge-builder, and a voice of reason calling us to build more bridges, or find the living ones spanning countless streams.

Burroughs is a vibrant voice in the wilderness coaxing us on, enticing us to find a way to cross whatever stream, whatever canyon, whatever range, whatever obstacle natural or artificial, with generous courage and genuine compassion.

2013

16

Ancoutahan

John Muir among Native Peoples. In recent times, Muir has been more intensely criticized for insensitive racial remarks. In some sense, this essay identifies a balance and context to understand Muir's observations without excusing his cultural limitations. This essay appears on the Sierra Club John Muir Exhibit website under "Biography."

Shall Brothers Be

The 19th and 20th centuries present a particularly tragic story of the systematic destruction of First Nations people on the American frontier. Tribes were decimated by war, seizure of land (facilitated by broken treaties), disease and cultural assimilation. While explorers, hunters and trappers were often first to make contact with indigenous inhabitants, opening the way for a flood of invaders, missionaries were particularly intent on transforming entire cultures through conversion, teaching English (primarily through Bible lessons), enforcing "proper" clothing and overall forcing native people to "conform, reform, or die."

Even though he resisted the forces that would restrict his own wildness, John Muir was steeped in a cultural mindset that allowed for this prejudice- powered injustice. It cannot be sugarcoated. He clearly viewed "Indians" as human but as primitive humans in need of knowledge, education and, to some extent, civilization. As Michael Cohen tries to explain this tension, *"Perhaps Muir's personal experience with the Indians was limited to the observation of decaying or degraded cultures. . . . If he was repulsed by wild Indians, he was also disappointed when he met an Indian who had become a shepherd and lost his wildness." (The Pathless Way*, 1984). No doubt Muir was caught in the contradictions of cultures. There were clear lapses in his thought now and then when he "lost his wildness" in judgement of those "wild ones" he knew so little about.

Having admitted these tensions, preconceptions and condescension in viewpoint, it can also be shown that Muir had at least some fascination, even admiration, for native cultures and their original relation to the natural world. If we are observant we can find in his writings a hesitant, though delighted, discovery of more than a non-human home in the solitary wilderness. To a degree, he found an unexpected welcoming among the human inhabitants of the wildlands as well.

Writing of the origins of Muir's mixed feelings about First Peoples that emerged from his early life in Wisconsin, Linnie Marsh Wolfe writes, "The American Indian was always a contradiction of John Muir's idea that wild humans should be clean and beautiful like wild animals" (*Son of the Wilderness*, 1945). Surely an odd concept for a "son of the wilderness." Wolfe explains that Muir was sickened in later life recalling how ancient grave-sites were plowed up on the farm to grow crops. In stark contrast to the violent ways settlers treated the land, he later wrote, "the Indians walk softly and hurt the landscape hardly more than the birds and squirrels" (My First Summer in the Sierra, 1911). Muir readers know that's a high complement coming from him.

As Donald Worster reasons, Muir understood that Indians "were a part of humankind. . .but people in general often depressed him by their frequent inability to harmonize with the rest of nature" (A *Passion for Nature*, 2008). He seemed to struggle with what he saw that disgusted him: how could people live so seamlessly, so intimately with the landscape yet be so hard to look at?

Throughout his life Muir had a keen interest in these mysterious people and offered many firsthand descriptions and insights in his observations of disintegrating and dying cultures. In *My First Summer in the Sierra* he describes a band of Mono Indians in stunning language: "They were wrapped in blankets made of the skins of sage-rabbits. The dirt on some of the faces seemed almost old enough and thick enough to have a geological significance." He goes on to say that he wanted to pass by the group but they surrounded him asking for tobacco and whisky. He was "glad to get away from the gray, grim crowd," yet after they moved on he reflected, "[It] seems sad to feel such desperate repulsion from one's fellow beings, however degraded. To prefer the society of squirrels and woodchucks to that of our own species must surely be unnatural." For a moment it's unclear whether he means his repulsion or the Indians toward him, but then the mountaineer appears to sense his own preference for the wild over being with his species, and the next lines reveal something more: "So with a fresh breeze and a hill or mountain between us I must wish them Godspeed and try to pray and sing with [Robert] Burns,

"It's coming yet, for a 'that, that man to man, the warld over, shall brothers be for a 'that." ("A Man's a Man for a 'That")

This is decidedly not the attitude of the missionaries known to Muir.

Later, his innate prejudices surface again when he comes upon the tribe harvesting wild rye seeds near Moraine Lake. *I fancy the bread made from it must be as good as wheat bread. . . . The women were evidently enjoying [the gathering] laughing and chattering and looking almost natural, though most Indians I have seen are not a whit more natural in their lives than we civilized whites.* Oddly, I think, he reacts to their "uncleanness." But even in this harsh appraisal the not-so-clean and not-so-natural Scotsman admits, "Perhaps if I knew them better I should like them better." Once again, not a typical response we might hear from a merchant or missionary!

Significantly, he spends time writing down his observations of their brush tents, tastes the berries they collect and seems mystified by their diet including larvae, rabbit, deer, sheep, sage hens, squirrels and pine nuts. He finds the pine nuts delicious, but also writes admiringly of the way "the squaws carry immense loads on their backs across the rough passes and down the range, making journeys of about forty or fifty miles each way." For the rugged mountain man, this seems astounding. In fact, Muir was never known to carry such a load on his treks through the highlands.

In his first summer saunter through his beloved Range of Light, Muir said he never felt loneliness. Though he may not have had his Indian encounters in mind, he said he *"never enjoyed grander company. The whole wilderness seems to be alive and familiar, full of humanity. The very stones seem talkative, sympathetic, brotherly. No wonder when we consider that we all have the same Father and Mother."* I find this particularly remarkable since his lofty words appear to echo those lines from Burns and harken back to his encounters with the "unnatural" and "unclean" brothers (and sisters) who make their homes in that living wilderness. Perhaps, as he scribbles later, he has been so filled with "wild enthusiasm" he cannot contain the overwhelming sense that "More and more, in a place like this, we feel ourselves a part of wild Nature, kin to everything"—even kinship with those we might like (and learn from) if we knew them better.

Tenaya and the Ahwahnee People of Yosemite

Before considering his formative times among Alaskan natives, it would be informative to consider Muir's historical record of the early history of White/Indian relations in *The Yosemite* (1914).

In an otherwise wonderful narrative, Muir stumbles when claiming the original inhabitants of the Valley made war upon the frenzy of gold miners, "in their usual murdering, plundering style." This is more than cringe-worthy bigotry. He explains how the government gathered the tribes onto reservations but the Yosemite (Grizzly Bear) Tribe "were the most troublesome and defiant of all."

In a great irony of history apparently completely lost on Muir, it was the rounding up of the tribe by a battalion under the command of Major Savage (!) that led to the Yosemite Valley being "discovered." You can't be more blind to the twisted lessons of history than this! And what was Major Savage's message to the people defending their own tribal lands? According to Muir, he told the Indians "if they would come in and make treaty" they would be provided with "protection" including food and clothing, but if they did not come in willingly, the Major would "make war upon them and kill them all."

The tribe responded in an amazing way. The chief, Tenaya, came alone to meet with the Major. This is where Muir shows another, more humane, side. He records the words of the old chief in an assumed respectful manner. The chief did not want anything from "the Great Father" because "the Great Spirit" is their father and they only wish to remain "in the mountains where we were born, where the ashes of our fathers have been given to the wind." Beautiful, powerful words. And recorded for all time by —John Muir.

Muir does not end with this story of the seizing of Yosemite and its people. The chief apologizes for the stealing of horses from the invaders and says he just wants peace. But the Major is firm. The tribe must leave. Muir spends several more pages weaving this awful tale of land stealing. Chief Tenaya finally gives up with these shaming words: "My heart has been sore. . .but I am now willing to go, for it is best for my people." As Muir lays it out, the valley was named Yosemite "to perpetuate the name of the tribe who so long had made their home there." Nevertheless, he adds, "The Indian name of the Valley, however, is Ahwahnee."

Some of the tribe resists the relocation. One of Tenaya's sons is killed escaping. The chief delivers himself and gives his final speech, recorded by, one might guess, a troubled Muir,

"Kill me, Sir Captain, yes, kill me as you killed my son, as

you would kill my people if they were to come to you. You would kill all my tribe if you had the power. Yes, Sir America, you can now tell your warriors to kill the old chief. . . . You may kill me, Sir Captain, but you shall not live in peace. I will follow in your footsteps. I will not leave my home, but be with the spirits among the rocks, the waterfalls, in the rivers and in the winds."

Muir goes on to relate that Tenaya never consented to sell the Valley. The chief was finally shot and killed after returning to the Valley. As Muir, perhaps with at least a smidgeon of sympathy, says it:" The Tenaya Canyon and lake were named for the famous old chief."

To one who has read a great deal of Muir's writings, the Yosemite occupation by "Sir America" can be heard echoing through a large part of the great naturalist's life and work. The preservationist who most loudly preached and proclaimed the protection of lands as wild, free sanctuaries belonging to no one and everyone, seemed almost haunted by the events that "opened" Yosemite and henceforward all National Parks.

One cannot excuse Muir for standing by somewhat dispassionately or forgive the United States Government for passionately stealing these lands and killing their original peoples like so much wild vermin. Yet I think it is informative and intriguing that John Muir was the scribe who told the true story while dedicating his life to calling us all "home" to these lands where "divinity" inhabits the rocks and waterfalls, rivers and winds—echoing the old chief.

In his journals, Muir offers hints of his conflicted feelings about First Peoples. "To the Indian mind all nature was instinct with deity. A spirit was embodied in every mountain, stream, and waterfall" (July, 1890). This comes close to a summary of Muir's own mind. Some years earlier the younger Muir had appreciated "the redmen, with flesh colored like the rocks, and sinews tough as the granite, who for thousands of years have dragged in files through these silent depths, clad in dull skins and grass, with mountain flowers stuck in their black hair and their wild animal eyes sparkling bright as the lakes" (1872). If this was not John Muir, I for one would think this was disrespectful and disparaging language. But it is hard not to imagine Muir himself revealing a not-so-hidden personal desire to join these wild ones in those silent depths. In fact, many would no doubt have described Muir emerging from the mountains in just such critical yet curious language (being as he was the dirty outdoorsman with sparkling bright eyes who never shaved!).

Muir's true feelings do not have to be read between the lines. Even when he pokes and teases, he can be rather straightforward. In a letter to his Wisconsin friend, Emily Pelton, written from Yosemite Valley in April 1872, he pointedly prepares her for an upcoming camping trip to Tenaya Canyon: "You mention the refining influences of society. Compared with the intense purity and cordiality and beauty of Nature, the most delicate refinements and cultures of civilization are gross barbarisms."

Using colorful language, he pushes back at her societal sensibilities, writing that he has no wish to have contact with the "rough vertical animals" who bring their "filth" into the "pure" mountains. Then he offers a self-description similar to how he portrays Indians he has encountered: "You'll find me rough as the rocks and about the same colour—granite ... . Come and see my teachers; come, see my Mountain Mother."

Alaska: Chief Shakes of the Stickeen

We cannot appreciate John Muir's unsettled and unsettling relationship with Native peoples without a close view of his Alaskan experience. As his climbing companion and devoted missionary, The Rev. Samuel Hall Young, says in *Alaska Days with John Muir* (1915): "Muir's mission was to find and study the forests, mountains and glaciers." They both enjoyed the same poets, such as Burns, and carried copies of Thoreau and Emerson. Only Rev. Young carried a Bible since "[Muir] had his in his head." One went to Alaska to preach to wild people and the other went to learn from the wilderness and preach a primal, wild gospel.

So it is that on his seven tramps into the northland of Alaska between 1879 and 1899, Muir was brought face to face with some of the most primitive of people who became, in some sense, the most profound examples of the Wild Life he longed for. On his earliest trips, in the company of Christian missionaries, Muir was introduced to Natives in the heartwrenching process of being converted by American Religion and American "Civilization." As Richard Nelson puts it in his introduction to Muir's *Travels in Alaska* (1997 intro to the 1915 book): *"John Muir was witness to a crucial time in the history of the Tlingit people: the very moment when their religious beliefs were being overturned and their entire culture was at the brink of profound change."* It is in this context that Muir, who was often careful to cite the Indian names to locations (Tahoma for Mount Rainier for instance), became a storyteller of more than ice and forests. He became the storyteller for flesh and blood human lives, recording and relating some of the most meaningful moments of wisdom as well as waste—waste of perfect opportunities to learn from the First Naturalists whose wisdom would soon be lost.

Muir quickly saw that Alaska was a special place. "To the lover of pure wildness Alaska is one of the most wonderful countries in the world." It didn't take him long to have his enthusiasm a bit tempered by the conflict of cultures. He was warned that "the Indians were a bad lot" and that the woods were "impenetrable." Being Muir, he took up the challenges.

"These natural difficulties made the grand wild country all the more attractive, and I determined to get into the heart of it." Perhaps he didn't anticipate that a portion of that heart would be found in his interactions with the original Alaskans.

His initial guides were missionaries, their families and their converts, so he stepped immediately into tours of mission schools and evangelical services on this frontier of faith. Always looking for opportunities to escape from the conversion business, both Whites and Natives thought the wild Scotsman was a strange sort, with his unbelievable and unheard-of mission, not to people in darkness but to the mountains of light.

The true spirit of Muir's admiring fascination with Native people and their culture is clear in the contrasts he observed vis-a-vis the "civilized" world. It could be said that he stepped out and beyond cultural prejudice as his experience brought him closer to the people themselves.

He was grateful that Rev. Young brought him into "confiding contact" with the Tlingit tribes so he could learn all about them. Their sense of family honor was particularly touching to Muir who thought that the "perfectly natural, straightforward way" they spoke of death was much healthier than "the vacant, silent, hesitating behavior of most civilized friends." Unlike the city-world, the tribes were unafraid to speak of death, "[sympathizing] with their neighbors in their misfortunes and sorrows." He also noted they were "fond and indulgent parents" who never spanked their children.

On Wrangell island in 1879 Muir was invited, along with three Presbyterian missionaries and their wives, to a dinner with chief Shakes of the Stickeen tribe (Wrangell sits at the mouth of the Stikine River flowing 400 miles from British Columbia). Muir commented that the dinner was good but "there was no trace of Indian dishes." The tribe gave Muir the name *Ancoutahan*. He was told it translated: "adopted chief." He felt privileged by the honor.

The visitors were entertained with traditional dances of the bear, porpoise and deer after which an Indian woman explained that they would never again dance in this "foolish way" since now they are no longer "blind" and "Jesus Christ tells us what to do." Muir was paying close attention to these words of new converts. Then he records the pathetic words of the chief who thanks the missionaries for bringing the light to the tribe who had lived in darkness, and through their gospel "taught us the right way to live and the right way to die." After the entertainment, the party of Whites was given the robes and headdresses that had been worn by tribal shamans. Muir received one himself.

Why would John Muir relate this story? What motivated the naturalist to pencil his account of the last tribal dances of the Stickeen people? There may be a hint in the words he chose about chief Shakes, who stood to address his converting conquerors "with grave dignity."

Muir re-tells the scene related by his missionary friend:

"When the missionary had finished his sermon, chief Shakes [of the Stickeens] slowly arose, and, after thanking the missionary for coming so far to bring them good tidings and taking so much unselfish interest in the welfare of this tribe, he advised his people to accept the new religion. . . .

'Compared with the white man we are only blind children, knowing not how best to live either here or in the country we go to after we die.... But I am too old to learn a new religion, and besides, many of my people who have died were bad and foolish people, and if this word the missionary has brought us is true, and I think it is, many of my people must be in that bad country the missionary calls 'Hell, 'and I must go there also, for a Stickeen chief never deserts his people in time of trouble ...' It's obvious that Muir exhibited a greater measure of respect for the chief than the learned "doctors of divinity."

As Muir made his way deeper into the Alaskan wilderness where he "found a home" he must have been haunted by the memories of his time among the Stickeen. When he speaks of hearing the "voice of God" in the "glorious temples" of the mountains, that he had "seen Him and heard Him preaching like a man" out in the "pure wildness," it is in distinct opposition, even defiant heresy, in the context of Christian mission activities and intents.

One "invented excursion" (mission) took Muir into an abandoned Stickeen village led by one missionary who was excited about finding artifacts that "the Indians aboard will dig for us." Muir's reflection is classic:

"It seemed strange, however, that so important a mission to the most influential of the Alaskan tribes should end in a deserted village. But divinity abounded nevertheless; the day was divine and there was plenty of natural religion in the newborn landscapes that were being baptized in sunshine, and sermons in the glacial boulders on the beach where we landed."

One imagines the journal-keeper keeping his mouth shut with these heretical musings! And, ironically, we can both fault Muir for his silence and applaud him for writing these "innocent" words that exposed his reading public to the tragic disappearance of those who also felt "at home" in Alaska.

As he saunters the sad village, Muir is struck with "the excellence of the workmanship" the "admirable geometry" the "completeness of form" and the "skill of a wild and positive kind." He was captivated. With his keen eye for detail, Muir takes some time studying the totems and their meaning in the life of the tribe, the "family pride" and the "truly wonderful" designs. There was a "venerable air" about the scene. He says that, like the Tlingit tribes, these totem poles are lifted with a great feast and dancing by a happy circle of people. "They are always planted firmly in the ground and stand fast, showing the sturdy erectness of their builders." Ancoutahan was unashamed to show his respect and admiration.

What happened next in this ghostly village shocked the sensitive saunterer from California. As Muir tells it:

"While I was busy with my pencil, I heard chopping going on at the north end of the village, followed by a heavy thud, as if a tree had fallen. . .The archaeological doctor called the steamer deck hands to one of the most interesting of the totems and directed them to cut it down. . .and convey it aboard the steamer, with a view to taking it on East to enrich some museum or other. This sacrilege came near causing trouble, and would have cost us dear had the totem not chanced to belong to the Kadachan family, the representative of which is a member of the newly organized Wrangell Presbyterian Church.

Kadachan looked very seriously into the face of the reverend doctor and [asked]: 'How would you like to have an Indian go to a graveyard and break down and carry away a monument belonging to your family?'

However, the religious relations of the parties and a few trifling presents embedded in apologies served to hush and mend the matter."

Muir concludes this awful story with an air of detachment. One could imagine he was stunned to silence, though he was not a man known for silence. He quickly brings this chapter to conclusion with a description of the "glorious sunset" that helped to "clear away the shadows of our meditations among the ruins." After the steamship lands back at Wrangell, he seems to nearly run back to his room with the throwaway comment that this episode was "one of the most memorable of my life."

Alaska: Chief Toyatte of the Chilcats

One other story to relate here concerns chief Toyatte of the Chilcats, "the most influential of all the Thlinkit tribes." Muir had already been hearing stories of the nobility and hospitality of the tribe. Reverend Samuel Young preached to an assembly of 250 in the Chilcat village. The chief expressed thanks, then invited Muir to speak. Muir was reluctant but when compelled simply explained that he was in the land to see the glaciers, mountains and forests. He ended up offering a mini-lecture on "the country God had given them" and "the brotherhood of man."
After further meetings over the days ahead, the shaman rose to speak with appreciative words ("the Indian and White man are on the same side of the river, eye to eye, heart to heart").

Muir was treated with great respect and hospitality almost to the point of embarrassment. His five speeches were so well received that he was offered wives, a church, school and other honors!

The other orator admired by Muir was chief Toyatte. The description we're given of the chief's indoctrination into the Presbyterian Church and his subsequent death speaks volumes on Muir's deep connection to the First Peoples of Alaska. At Fort Wrangell, after Toyatte had spoken of his mother's religion, the shamans and his new faith, Muir wrote:

"In all his gestures, and in the language in which he expressed himself, there was a noble simplicity and earnestness and majestic bearing which made the sermons and behavior of the three distinguished divinity doctors present seem commonplace in comparison."

When Muir returned to Wrangell he learned the old man had been killed in a tribal dispute. Once again, Muir's pencil is as active as a walking stick, as we hear how Toyatte protected Rev. Young and refused to be taken to a safe place in the church:

"[Toyatte said], 'Mr. Young, I am not going to fight. . .I must stay with my young men and share their dangers. . . but I will not fight. But you must go away; you are a minister and you are an important man. Go to your home in the fort.'

Toyatte was shot and killed. Muir ends this poignant event with these memorial words:

"On this first Alaska excursion I saw Toyatte under all circumstances. . .but never under any circumstances did I ever see him do anything, or make a single gesture, that was not dignified, or hear him say a word that might not be uttered anywhere. He often deplored the fact that he had no son to take his name at his death, and expressed himself as very grateful when I told him that his name would not be forgotten—that I had named one of the Stickeen glaciers for him."

And, of course, had written of the noble chief's life and tragic death in his last book, *Travels in Alaska*.

A Native in Nature

In his first published book, *The Mountains of California* (1894), Muir finds companions in the highcountry who share his appreciation for the beauty of birds. Unlike apathetic lowlanders, the Digger Indians he meets tell him their names for wild flowers while their children "gather and braid them as decorations for their hair." This primal love is familiar to the bounding botanist.

Muir can, and ought to be, questioned for many of his anglo-centric views and prejudices toward First Nations people. It can certainly be argued that "Muir never managed to integrate completely the figure of Native [Humanity] into his ecological vision of the American wilderness" (Cohen, p. 189), but it cannot be denied, and ought not to be forgotten, that with his pencil in hand he preserved not only a written record of a vanishing culture but, as a zealous missionary of the ice-mountains, he helped to preserve the vast lands where he found home, among his new friends in the wilderness.

Returning to his beloved Sierra temples in 1874, he writes to his good friend, Jeanne Carr, describing an evening on horseback weaving through "the grand priest-like pines." He tells of a "strange mass of tones" carried on the breeze through the trees. His riding companion tells Muir that it's a death chant. "Some Indian is dead." They see fires shining red through the forest, "marking the place of congregation." He felt an "indescribable impressiveness" while he "listened eagerly." He sensed the swells of sorrow were as natural as the world he loved: "falling boulders and rushing streams and wind tones caught from rock and tree were in [the chanting]."

As they ride back into the night, Muir reflects: "I wondered that so much of mountain nature should well out from such a source." He seemed to long for that depth of identity with Nature.

On his 800-mile canoe trip in Alaska (1879), to the uncharted Glacier Bay and beyond, the crew consisted of four Stickeen (including Toyatte), Rev. Young and Muir. The "Ice Chief" as he was known to them, heard many stories from the guides:

"I greatly enjoyed the Indian's camp-fire talk this evening on their ancient customs, how they were taught by their parents ere the whites came among them, their religion, ideas connected with the next world, the stars, plants, the behavior and language of animals under different circumstances, manner of getting a living, etc."

As Wolfe says:" Muir was deeply impressed [that to the Indian mind all Nature was divine]. . .and "with his own deep-seated paganism, felt these children of the wilderness came nearer to the truth. . .than did the tutored, civilized exponents of Christianity."

It would be hard to read the words of the "Ice Chief" without sensing a certain warmth he felt toward his indigenous northern friends.

To conclude, there is one beautiful image that perhaps captures the true heart of Muir among Native People. On the canoe trip north among the Hootsenoo, Muir stayed overnight in a village called Killisnoo. The chief invited the explorers to sleep under his own roof with his family. Muir was delighted, saying, "I never felt more at home. The lovingkindness bestowed on the little ones made the house glow."

2014 (revised 2018)

17

Nearer to Wonder

Specifically a response to "Old Trees, Stardust, and Moments of Wonder: An Introduction to Religious Naturalism," by Rex Hunt

Sometime in February of 1867, Emerson scribbled in his journal that when he used words like "God" or "soul" these were "not part of any system, but spontaneous, and the nearest word I could find to the thing." When considering the dirt and the divine, soil and the sacred, earthly and heavenly things, we might keep Emerson's guideline in mind. We're really on the search for words, ways to incarnate our experiences in language. And we often blunder in the wonder—we speak too soon, calling attention to ourselves, our beliefs about the world, instead of paying closer attention to what's there—the world in the raw, naked, without the shaming clothes of beliefs.

In his presentation of Religious Naturalism (full disclosure: I've been a member of the online Religious Naturalist Association for several years), Hunt chooses convenient terms like sacred, spiritual and of course God, though we find those placeholders hot and slippery to handle. "Placeholders"—that's perhaps the word I've been looking for myself. Like Emerson, we simply don't know what to say, what to call something or some experience, so we reach for the "nearest word" that seems to fit. That's human, natural. Yet, we ought to admit the inadequacy of our words and the fact that nonsense is not natural—we make up words to stand for something we imagine. We pick a placeholder.

The writer claims we are "enmeshed in nature," linked in a "web," and "we are the universe in the form of a human … the universe reflecting on itself." This holds a degree of attraction for me and I'm intrigued by the images. And yet, we see shapeless shadows of the old anthropomorphisms. Hunt asserts: "Such naturalistic wonder and awe counts as deeply spiritual." Does it? Remove the latter part of that sentence and we are left with naturalistic wonder and awe, and that "counts" as is, does it not? Deeply emotive, perhaps, but no "spirituality" necessary.

Sauntering in nearby Great Smoky Mountains National Park my wife and I are grateful to find well-maintained, well-marked trails. We need the signs; the first inhabitants did not. Others flout any regard for "Leave No Trace" by carving their names into trees or defacing rocks. I sometimes think of Religion that way. There is a tendency to deface the world, mark it up with distracting signs. We can't seem to help defacing a world—a universe—with our own faces. In doing this we disrespect both nature and ourselves.

Consider the assortment of "ologies" and "isms," particularly theisms. These can, if we're not careful, restrict our thinking and our expressions of our experience. I propose that what we are really talking about with these slippery spiritual semantics is what we may call *Wonderism* (or Wonderology). We are filled with wonder—wonder full—and the words come spilling out but we literally don't know what we're saying; all we know to say, if we have to say anything (and we don't, you know), is something about "spiritual things." But there are no spiritual "things," only ideas in our heads and they just don't correspond to what's there, what we see and hear and feel in moments of wonder. We are caught up in Wonderism and turn it into a babbling stream of meaningless words that somehow feel meaningful— because they're "supposed" to feel meaningful; that's what we've been hoodwinked to believe.

In Chile during his voyage on the Beagle (1834), Charles Darwin wrote: "I took several long walks while collecting objects of natural history ... I did not cease from wonder." Arriving in San Salvador (1836), Darwin wrote: "When quietly walking along the shady pathways, and admiring each successive view, one wishes to find language to express one's ideas. Epithet after epithet is found too weak to convey ... the sensation of delight which the mind experiences."

Darwin and Emerson identify our dilemma—how we describe our world delights or distracts. And we ought to be suspicious of those descriptions. Accuracy is important and actually elicits an indescribable delight (a phrase John Muir used). For the scientific or naturalist mind, an analysis of what is presented before their senses is worthy of wonder. Epithets may be weak and we wish to find language—accurate, descriptive, true language—to express what we see and how we see it.

What I suppose I've been preparing to say here is this: Religion replaced God and God replaced Nature. Nature must be restored to its rightful place, above all religion—even "naturalized" religion—, above any god. Religion destroys Wonder. It blocks our view; screens our perceptions. By laying traps for wonder, Religion attempts to capture it in the "holy" (set apart), in boxes of belief called holy spaces or holy scriptures, guarded by nonsensical words like "sacred," "divine" and "spiritual." All the while, the Wild, the wildness, the wilderness—full of wonder, saturated with wonder—runs free, impossible to dominate or domesticate. We could truly say Religion replaced God and God replaced Nature, as we wandered off the trail of truth, lost our way in the forest of faith.

In an essay on "Nature" (1844), Emerson poetically reflects on the wind in the trees and fields, the crackling of pine logs in a fire, and concludes: "These are the music and pictures of the most ancient religion." His interest is centered in the "original beauty" in nature, marred by "the poorness of our invention" and the "ugliness" of our cities and impositions upon the natural world. Emerson was identifying a kind of religion behind Religion—something much deeper in fact, and yet, like the beauty presented by his senses, it is a religion that needs no "poorness of invention," no religion or religious language.

I follow the conversations of Religious Naturalists because it's clear they seek to appeal to progressive believers as well as "spiritually intrigued" scientists, naturalists and philosophers who are seeking to "discover the sacred" in nature. This might be understood as a step toward Emerson's "most ancient religion." However, I no longer find that satisfying or, frankly, all that honest. Labeling nature, or essential parts of nature, with ancient supernatural terms, does that same thing the old theologies do: attracts and distracts up, up and away from the world as physical world and nature as material nature. We don't hear wind in the trees, the songs of the birds or crickets, or the crackle of the fire; we hear "spiritual" things, and we, and our world, are much poorer for it.

When Hunt lays out the four perspectives of "G-O-D" I quickly see I don't accept any of them. Though during one stage of my emergence from theism I was comfortable with a pantheistic or panentheistic view, I personally don't find a home with that thinking, no ground beneath my feet. Religious Naturalism as presented here, may be a step forward from traditional religious paths or a kind of backward step toward the intrinsic interrelationships practiced by indigenous peoples (most ancient religions?), yet I'm still left wondering where this is taking us. As Hunt says: "Nature can be a focus of religious attention." Yes, it can, and has been for a long time in many cultures. Yet, all my questions remain and boil down to the most fundamental: Why isn't nature enough to invite our attention and excite our wonder? In my mind, it is.

Scientific activity engages questions great and small, investigating, studying, naming, reaching tentative conclusions—and this process can seem like a cold box to package wonder in too. But the mission of the investigative mind is qualitatively different from the mission of the religious will. As Harvard biologist E.O. Wilson writes: "The cost to society as a whole of the bowed head has been enormous" (*The Meaning of Human Existence*). Nature does not need and cannot ask for worship or any kind of "reverence." We have to lift up our heads, open our eyes, and look nature directly in the eye (the beetle, the bird, the elephant, the orca, the storm, the black hole) and not allow ourselves the sleight of hand or slight of mind that would make of nature a sanctuary with spiritual furniture resting on super-natural semantics.

Closing out his argument, Hunt presents the possibility of religiously-inclined naturalists to create new "rituals and practices ... communal celebrations." That could be interesting to see, though a walk in the woods could accomplish something similar— if we're paying attention (not necessarily "religious attention"). At the conclusion, the writer offers an encapsulated definition or summary of RN: It is "an emergent religious ethical orientation." I understand. But this is one trail I can't take, because I've taken it before, and simply can't hike it again.

2020

18

Mini-Migrations

Written for the Rational Doubt blog on Patheos, this essay was composed in the naturalistic context of the Covid pandemic.

In this time of pandemic, I often reflect on what is endemic to our worldviews. What is the lens we see through, and do we even have "the eyes to see and ears to hear" what is really happening around us and in us?

I tend to turn to wise voices in history who exhibit a wiser, wider and wilder outlook on things—which quite naturally means a deeper "in-look" at things as well. They speak to the Big Picture while bringing it home to the human species and our minuscule part in the nature of things.

Are we willing to face up to how small we are, how powerless, how much we're not in control? By the way, this is a question for all of us, religious or secular.

One of the most inspiring passages in the entire "Gospel of John Muir" concerns the self-importance of humans:

"The world, we are told, was made especially for [humanity]—a presumption not supported by all the facts." (*A Thousand-Mile Walk to the Gulf*, 1916)

Muir goes on to expose the arrogant brand of theology that assumes all animals are placed on the planet for our use and consumption. Sheep, whales, plants are all here "for us." But then Muir turns the tables. What about predators? What was God's plan with lions, alligators, bears, sharks (viruses!)—those creatures who can be deadly to human beings?

"Now, it never seems to occur to these far-seeing teachers that Nature's object in making animals and plants might possibly be first of all the happiness of each one of them, not the creation of all for the happiness of one." He continues his freethought sermon in the face of the orthodox preachers:

"Why should man value himself as more than a small part of the one great unit of creation? And what creature of all that the Lord has taken the pains to make is not essential to the completeness of that unit—the cosmos?"

Thus our secular saint brings us to this startling, stunning sentence:

"The universe would be incomplete without [humanity]; but it would also be incomplete without the smallest transmicroscopic creature that dwells beyond our conceitful eyes and knowledge."

I've seen a copy of *The Origin of Species* in the Muir house in Martinez, California. Though Muir carried the Bible in his head from early memorization, he also carried Darwin, Humboldt and the poetry of Robert Burns in his active brain. He was a man of science and skepticism, though he still had a "Lord" in his life (often using "God" and "Nature" interchangeably). He wasn't stuck in books though, holy or otherwise. He absorbed the world through his senses and responded as a student, with down-to-earth common sense and logic.

So here we have Muir—the mountain man who felt that he was endemic in Nature and the natural world was intrinsic to him. One use of the word *endemic* relates to a plant or animal that is "native and restricted to a certain place." In this sense, Muir, in fact all human beings, are native to certain places—and, we might say, native to the earth itself.

Yet think of migration—the migrant movements of living things across the planet. As *National Geographic* describes it, "Many animal species migrate, including species of fish, crustaceans, amphibians, reptiles, insects, and mammals. These animals might journey by land, sea, or air to reach their destination, often crossing vast distances and in large numbers" (https://www.nationalgeographic.org/encyclopedia/migration/). And while migration is often a return trip, emigration is moving to new habitation, relocating to a new home (a good or bad journey for human migrants as well).

Enter one way of viewing viruses. As Muir reminded us, even the smallest of microscopic critters is a critical part of the whole picture, the complete natural creation. So, as creepy as it may sound, and as tragic as it may prove to our one species among all, a virus is an animal on the move, using us for transportation, and maybe killing us along the way. It means us no harm; there is no intention to sicken or kill, of course. But we still speak of "fighting a war" against these innocent "beasts" on the attack. We're put on the defensive.

Would it help to re-frame a pandemic in this way, on this micro-level? No doubt there will be resistance, even as we try to build our resistance to the infection.

We may find another image helpful, or not: When Henry Thoreau was returning from a river journey with his older brother John in 1839, he was reflecting on what may await them back in Concord. Maybe they would find seasonal work as autumn began, or,

"Perhaps Nature would condescend to make use of us even without our knowledge, as when we help to scatter her seeds in our walks, and carry burs and cockles on our clothes from field to field" (*A Week on the Concord and Merrimack Rivers*, 1849).

But what if we did have knowledge, we were aware of what Nature is doing, of how Nature is using us to navigate and propagate? Would we happily participate in the fecundity, the endless process of new life on the planet? Maybe we would … if it didn't kill us!

Like all predators we want to kill this one before it kills us. It's our grizzly, our wolf, our rattlesnake, our great white. Because we don't know how to tame it, we fear it, defend against it, and wipe it out—if we can. Or, we somehow find a way to co-exist with it, to live with our fear and manage it—if we can. And maybe we can't always overcome that greatest of all our fears: *our powerlessness.*

I suppose a main lesson we have presented here is that we are participants in the pageant, even the deadly parade, the migration and emigration endemic to who we are. Humanity should keep in mind the significant but "small part" we play in the creative drama that is forever permeated (infected?) with the terrifying potential for destruction and death.

Medical professionals tell us we always have viruses in our bodies (viruses may be more numerous than stars in the universe! https://www.nationalgeographic.com/science/2020/04/factors-allow-viruses-infect-humans-coronavirus/). They are residents sharing the human hotel. Biologists tell us we are made of a living soup of cells—bone, blood and brain in a watery broth of bacteria. Makes you proud to be human? I wonder. But maybe we ought to be proud, content to be hosting so many "guests" at one time and, generally, we all get along fairly well!

To be honest, maybe we should be proud of our soupy species and grateful for our wild, animal nature, while at the same time humbled by the humus we emerged from—the same teeming soil where viruses also live and move and have being.

2020

19

Praying Down the Tornado

Originally published on State of Formation *(Journal of Inter-religious Dialogue)*

I used to be a "prayer warrior." One youth group leader in High School cried after I prayed one evening. "I wish I could pray like you," she sobbed. I sure knew how to talk to the Lord and, alongside a small group of other students, we were sure we could "move the hand of God." We prayed in churches (Evangelical, Pentecostal, Baptist, Presbyterian, Campus Crusade, House Churches and more); we prayed at school, we prayed on the beach, prayed at home, prayed while we drove, prayed while we read our bibles and brushed our teeth. We "prayed in the Spirit," "prayed in tongues," sang and sat in circles of intercession and confession and praise and supplication. We did it all. And God spoke with us all the time. Oh yes He did!

Those prayer-saturated days are over now. I gave up prayer a number of years ago. It wasn't that prayer didn't "work," because it did! Prayer always re-assured me that I had a Friend, a Protector, that was bigger and stronger than any force in the universe. Prayer was my security blanket, my shield, my storm shelter. . . until it didn't work.

I gave up praying when I woke up to realize it was really "all about Me." The conversation was all one-sided. Now wait. I always prayed for others. I constantly asked the Creator of the Universe to "help" and to "be present with" and to "protect" and to "guide" just about everyone I met. Even during the years I was an interfaith chaplain with people excluded from most communities and congregations (poor and mentally ill folk, prisoners and people of the street) I was continually asked to "pray for" someone, something, somewhere. I learned it was better to use less words, to breathe and to sit with people. That was "prayer enough." But I had to be honest: prayer was really for me. Not for others, not for God. Prayer was once all about Me-and-God, then prayer was all about what Others needed. A noble progression, maybe. But finally I had to be honest: prayer, in whatever form, was about me.

Have you noticed that just about every time you hear someone talking about "talking with God" it's pretty much all about them, about the pray-er? The Almighty Lord of All is listening to them and every little detail of their lives is of special concern to the Lord (Allah, Krishna, Buddha, Father, Goddess, any Lord will do). Except, isn't it odd that they have to keep asking for help with ceaseless worshipping or praising or thanking? Prayer seems to be a perpetually spiraling twister that can cut lives and communities apart. Doesn't anyone find it strange that someone has to ask for help or protection or healing from a Big Someone whose resume presumably includes a line about "loving, caring, all-present, all-powerful savior"? We once believed our prayerful devotions could "move the hands of God" but why did those heavenly hands wait for US to ask? (I know, some say it's a test, or a lesson or about trust and letting go. . .I know, that just makes no sense to me anymore, especially when we're talking about disease, death, destruction or disaster).

From what we hear, the people of Oklahoma (maybe a majority of inhabitants of the U.S. Southern states) are prayer warriors. Now, I mean no disrespect for how suffering people handle their suffering. But from what I've heard, the people of OK sure know how to pray. They know how to speak to God and "He listens." They pray for rain and it rains. They pray for protection and they're protected. Oh, sorry, am I'm missing something? I heard some say, "God protected me and mine; we prayed so hard and we were saved," while just across what used to be a street, others say, "God took my child and my house; the Lord giveth and the Lord taketh." Other, more liberal praying folk say things like "Storms are natural; we pray that people are safe." The most liberal (I was one of these) can say, "Prayer is to stand with the people; to pray is to rebuild." I understand. I just don't see the point anymore.

If prayer is a "relationship" with *the Great One Who Gives a Damn* (and a Blessing), then it seems, I mean it really appears, that—and I'm sorry to say it—there seems to be only one person relating with themselves. I mean, "prayer works" for some sometimes but not always and "prayer doesn't work" for others so it's reshaped into "Well, God's ways are mysterious and His purposes are. . . we don't know; but we love Him anyway because He loves us, even when we pray He protects children and a bunch of them die huddled in a school." This makes me think of some teachers in that public school in Moore who said they had kids singing "Jesus loves me" while their world was crashing down on them. Some didn't make it. Didn't Jesus love them?

I propose a simple (but risky) way to prove once and for all, that prayer really works. I suggest an ultimate test of prayer–not just praying, or one style of praying, but a test of Prayer itself. This isn't really meant to prove one way or another that a God exists. It's about a kind of spiritual Consumer Report on a product sold as safe and effective. Let's, once and for all, show that prayer is as real and effective as billions on our planet say it is.

Here's what I'd like to see. It would truly be an amazing event. We gather all the Warriors of Prayer, all the television evangelists, all the new breed of preacher politicians, all the biblical scholars and theologians, all the praying conservatives and liberals, all the people who believe "prayer changes things" or alters world events or really does anything at all. Bring all these folks to the next town, like Moore, OK, when the forecasters are issuing their predictions and the sirens are sounding (people in Moore had a few days warning). All the "people of prayer" will circle the city, hold hands and pray in any and all the ways they choose. They can sing and squeeze the holy book of their choice. They can dance and yell or meditate in silence.

As the twister (or tsunami or quake or firestorm or whatever) approaches, they could all pull in tight and surround the school full of kids, hundreds of frightened children hugged by their courageous teachers. And the crowd prays like there was no tomorrow. Now, this *Ultimate Prayer Circle* (UPC, like a FEMA of Faith) would boldly and without fear face down that tornado with every prayer possible. They would stand their ground, standing firm on their faith, "claim the Name" and "lean on the everlasting arms." As the towering beast approached, they would not move, forming a Wall of Prayer. If any time was Miracle Time, this is it.

What could we expect? Imagine this. The dust and debris settles. Silence descends. The tornado has roared passed. The town is gone, the circle is decimated, scripture pages swirling in the wind. . .or are they? Maybe the circle still stands. Maybe the school is intact, the children are safe and emerge into the sunshine. Maybe everyone falls to their knees or leaps for joy and the herds of media hounds, cameras rolling, stand silently, for once, in awe. All is well. The *Ultimate Prayer Circle* successfully convinced the Greatest Power in the Universe (aka God of Love) to stop the wind, what to Him (or Her) is nothing more than a bit of dust kicked up into the air (remember, Jesus "calmed the wind" and later said "greater things will you do").

A huge open-air worship service spontaneously forms with thousands and then millions streaming in, like a new field of dreams, with CNN and NBC and FOX and NPR all covering the event, full of love for each other and the God Who is *Lord of Tornadoes*. Everyone's in tears and everyone, even the hardest shell atheist, becomes a no-doubt believer. The UPC becomes the best —really the only–response to any disaster about to happen on the planet. As an arm of the newly formed United (in Prayer) Nations, their leaders fly all around the world to face down anything anywhere, natural or unnatural disaster, with their protective wall of prayer.

I'd like to see that. Really. Then skeptics like me, who once believed so strongly in the power of prayer, who prayed countless passionate prayers as pastoral leaders, will have to simply shut up and sit back dumbfounded, shaking our heads at the awesomeness and effectiveness of proven faith-based prayer. We would, I would, have to say, "Well, I guess it's not all about me, it's about prayer, it's about faith, it's about a real Creator who controls the Cosmos, who cares, who listens, who protects. . .if only we ask." And we'll be forced to admit, to confess, that all "tornadoes" of any kind–cancer and violence and war and everything–can be fought back by the Wall of Prayer. The Secular has fallen to the Sacred; defeated, finally, by The Wall.

The possibilities have my head spinning.

Postscript. We're sorry and sad to say we can imagine a very different result. The prayer circle, in fact hundreds of prayer circles, millions and billions of prayers from people of every faith in every country on earth, couldn't stop the storm, the tsunami, the fire, the earthquake. People died, hundreds, even thousands of children died, or were horribly injured, or lost their families. Years and years of "acts of God" faced with acts of Prayer. . . Years and years of unanswered prayers, pleas, begging for help. The warriors of prayer swept away with nothing left but silence and pain and suffering and. . .something wonderful came of this tornado: people helping others rebuild their homes and their lives and their hopes; undistracted by supernatural supplications, they work together to prepare as best they can for personal and community disasters, with thoughtful, reasonable discussion based on experience, with wise leadership and good sense.

Though the UPC was literally blown away, people know they have each other; they are grounded in their goodness and the overwhelming power of compassion and lovingkindness. They have re-discovered the timeless truth: with no guarantees in the face of the immense power of Nature, the resilient human community can face any storm as a common circle that is, time and again, its own shelter

2013

20

Whitman's Divinity

And The Poet became flesh and dwelt among us. Thus we may read in the natural gospel if published in July of 1855. To the delight of Ralph Waldo Emerson, a young New York printer appeared as the true representative voice, the native singer whom America—perhaps the world—had been waiting for. He exemplified the one "who sees through the flowing vest the firm nature, and can declare it," the one who proclaims "the new religion," the one "whom all things await." For Emerson, the author of *Leaves of Grass* understood that "America is a poem … that dazzles the imagination" ("The Poet").

Walt Whitman (1819-1892). Naturalist John Burroughs called him "The Poet of the Cosmos." Vilified and censored in his day, largely ignored in our day. A mysterious man with little mystery left after piles of biographies and analyses. People are still curious, most often curious about his sexual orientation or exploits. Criticized for his self-absorption, his ego, his wildness and heretical views. Who should care about the old Grey Poet?

It is my view that Whitman, the man and the work, offers a critical contribution to individual and communal identities, national politics and secularized-spiritual understandings. It is the latter that I wish to focus on here. People of faith would do well to listen to Whitman's words and the "incarnate word" of his life. And non-theists would greatly benefit from a closer look at this explorer of ideas. He was a free-thinking prophet, a bridge-maker beyond belief and a guide for any who dare to saunter down the open road beyond the fields of faith. If ever a person showed us how to venture out Beyond God, Walt Whitman is the poet, the person and the preacher of the more excellent way.

Representative lines from the Representative Poet:

"What do you suppose I would intimate to you in a hundred ways, but that man or woman is as good as God? And that there is no God any more divine than Yourself? And that that is what the oldest and newest myths finally mean?" ("Laws for Creations," Autumn Rivulets)

"Why, who makes much of a miracle? As to me I know of nothing else but miracles. . . To me every hour of the light and dark is a miracle, Every cubic inch of space is a miracle, Every square yard of the surface of the earth is spread with the same." ("Miracles," Autumn Rivulets)

"Young man I think I know you–I think this face is the face of the Christ himself, dead and divine and brother of all, and here again he lies." ("A Sight in Camp in the

Daybreak Gray and Dim," Drum-Taps)

"Or Time and Space, Or shape of Earth divine and wondrous. . .Be ye my Gods." ("Gods," By the Roadside)

"Yet underneath Socrates clearly see, and underneath Christ the divine I see, The dear love of man for his comrade, the attraction of friend to friend. . ." ("The Base of All Metaphysics," Calamus)

"We two, how long we were fool'd, Now transmuted, we swiftly escape as Nature escapes, We are Nature, long have we been absent, but now we return. . ." ("We Two, How Long We Were Fool'd," Children of Adam)

"Spontaneous me, Nature. . ." ("Spontaneous Me," Children of Adam)

"And if the body were not the soul, what is the soul?. . . If anything is sacred the human body is sacred. . ." ("I Sing the Body Electric," Children of Adam)

"And I have said that the soul is not more than the body, And I have said that the body is not more than the soul, And nothing, not God, is greater to one than one's self is. . .And I say to humankind, Be not curious about God, For I who am curious about each am not curious about God. . . I hear and behold God in every object, yet understand God not in the least, Nor do I understand who there can be more wonderful than myself. . . Why should I wish to see God better than this day?" ("Song of Myself," 48)

"My faith is the greatest of faiths and the least of faiths." ("Song of Myself," 43)

"Divine am I inside and out, and I make holy whatever I touch or am touch'd from, The scent of these arm-pits aroma finer than prayer, This head more than churches, bibles, and all the creeds." ("Song of Myself," 24)

"Good in all. . .To be this incredible God I am! To have gone forth among other Gods, these men and women I love. . .O amazement of things–even the least particle! O spirituality of things!" ("Song at Sunset," Songs of Parting)

"Chanting the square deific, out of the One advancing. . .Life of the great round world, the sun and stars, and of man, I, the general soul, Here the square finishing, the solid, I the most solid, Breathe my breath also through these songs." ("Chanting the Square Deific," Whispers of Heavenly Death)

"We consider bibles and religions divine–I do not say they are not divine, I say they have all grown out of you, and may grow out of you still, It is not they who give the life, it is you who give the life, Leaves are not more shed from the trees, or trees from the earth, than they are shed out of you." ("A Song for Occupations," 3)

Was Whitman a believer in any recognizable religious sense? Did he believe in God at all? Was his God simply a sense of divinity absorbed into the cosmos, a poetically playful as well as intellectually rigorous pantheism? Questions we probe and scan over the body of the man and his writings (the tree and his "leaves") reveal a complex person who was both a product of his 19th Century context and a person who simply and profoundly chose to step outside of the mainstream of that context—to create, as it were, his own context. How did he do that? This is perhaps the greatest question that will bring us back time and again to the poet's beyond-spiritual experience, his secular vocation.

Whitman, as represented in the quotations above, blended an intense understanding of the divine and sacred into an extreme experience of immersion into radical culture. Whether spending time with the "cab" drivers on the streets of New York City, editing newspapers, working as a clerk in the Patent Office in Washington, D.C. or ambling into the fields or forests to write poems, this spiritual explorer and pathfinder opened up new insights into the human person that placed the person at the center of an equally "sacred" community, nation, world and universe. Poetry can do that! Yet, for the man from Paumanok (Long Island), poetry was closer to the original vision of that activity: a solid, participatory relation with the environment (the surrounding circle of life) indistinguishable, inseparable from active creation of one's environment.

As a "poem" was a "making or doing" for the Greeks, so the poem for Whitman was an embodying of life itself right in the center of the whirlpool of all existence. For him, the body and the soul were one. Plain and simple. No separate existence. And "soul" for the poet was great and divine while equally ordinary, commonplace and definitely not other-worldly or even super-natural.

Whitman was pre-eminent among all modern poets as a realist, a very this-worldly incarnation of Person-hood, the Self, the I and the I Am, without much of any hint at a "transcendent" unless that meant a context-ualizing of the Individual, the concrete grounding of the universal sense of Individual or Self (I do not con-sider Whitman a member of the Transcendentalist camp, yet he certainly bivouacked in the general area of the wide and wild frontiers. He packed his well-worn tent with a vast self-reliance, crisscrossing the pathways of Emerson and his club, without "camp-ing out" too near their more acceptable and warming campfire).

Did his singing of the universalized Self, balanced with the particularized Self make Whitman a kind of Westernized Hindu or Buddhist? Not precisely. No more than Emerson or Thoreau (Emerson exclaimed of Whitman's *Leaves*: "The best piece of American Buddhism ... American to the bone ... a mixture of the Bhagavad Gita and the New York Herald"). There are elements woven into his work that seem to bow to the East but they are strands and threads (or leaves) he casts into his green and growing field of poems. They are intriguing images for him and help him do what he is best at: throwing open the doors and win-dows of the mind (body, soul, spirit. . .Self), breaking the barriers of East and West (Orient/Occident as well as American bifurcation) to "do" what all great poetry "does"–embodies creative expression and evolution.

What would Whitman say his "spirituality" or "religion" was? I think he's fairly clear about this. *"My faith is the greatest of faiths and the least of faiths,"* he warbles in "Song of Myself." He was encompassing, radically inclusive and used the language of faith to scatter the seeds of belief and unbelief in the same field. His "leaves of grass" were planted and nourished on Civil War battlefields as well as country lanes and city boulevards. His written words were grown organically from the blood of young men, North and South, the scars of slaves, erotic exploration, the questions of children and all that made his world meaningful. His words were rooted in reality and nurtured in the free and open air breathed by all–mingled with breezes from the battlefields and the injustices wrought by political and religious machinery.

In a literal way practiced by few before or since, this man, this poet, this American Soul (poetic nature), wandered and wondered among common people and the "great" (commoners with a name and position), settlers, slaves, soldiers and others who were never left faceless or meaningless. Whitman was present, fully, to record the commonest events as having uncommon significance and universal meaning.

I often think of Whitman, especially during the War years, as a "chaplain." His volunteer service in the hospitals, especially in Washington, exemplifies everything I learned in twenty-five years of interfaith chaplaincy. In *Specimen Days* as well as in the "dark" poems of "Drum-Taps" this man reveals a completely immersed human being who was unafraid of the suffering of strangers. In the light of my long experience immersed in the dark and forgotten places where most fear to tread, I can only conclude that Walt Whitman was, in every meaningful way, a chaplain of the highest caliber—a "model of ministry," as we studied in seminary.

What does this image of Whitman as chaplain present to us? A very confusing picture! Especially if one is either a narrow theist or a narrow non-theist. The confusion is highly productive here! In "Laws for Creations" the poet expounds his earth-shaking, belief-rattling sensibility:

"What do you suppose I would intimate to you in a hundred ways, but that man or woman is as good as God? And that there is no God any more divine than Yourself? And that that is what the oldest and newest myths finally mean?"

Alright. Every one is "divine;" all is "sacred." Then what? What does religion do with that? What does science do? Sink into it. All he says is: this is me, the poems, the experiences, the life, thought and meditation ... these are all me, and they are you, if you pick up and read this book, this life in paper and ink and blood and brains. We live the Civil War and slavery and the assassination of Lincoln with Whitman. And we live the crossing of passengers on Brooklyn Ferry and the singing of birds and the passages of a lifetime in the songs of this one representative poet.

In the very experience of life and living, of walking into the temples and terrors and smelling the scent of death mingled with the scent of a lover by a river, we come alive and in that emergence we strangely, uncomfortably welcome the release of "faith" and "unfaith" of "my side and your side," and there is the wondrous, the "miracle" that makes everything a "miracle"—our common, earthly acceptance of one profound troubling fact: we are compost.

"Something startles me," the poet admits. The earth is terrifying but wonderful in its power to cleanse all the refuse, all the diseased corpses, recycled and renewed by the earth. "Behold this compost! behold it well!," he preaches. "What chemistry!," he teaches. "It distills. . .It renews. . .It gives such divine materials to people, and accepts such leavings from them at last" ("This Compost," Autumn Rivulets).

Whitman is divine, if divine means "connected to the vine," the intertwined relationships that behold the compost, that hold the cosmos together (the threads, strands, strings, chemistry). And he reminds us of our divinity, the "sacred secularity" of all life. And this does to faith and religion what few have the ability to do: transforms it all, absorbs, recycles and renews into compost to grow something better, something greater.

Whitman not only prepared the way, he brought the

gospel, the holy book—the only one that brings life because it is Life: *Nature*.

"We are Nature, long have we been absent, but now we return." This is our conversion, our salvation, our own terrestrial, natural divinity.

2015

ABOUT THE AUTHOR

Chris Highland was born and raised in the Seattle area, then lived in the San Francisco Bay Area for over three decades. He has degrees from Seattle Pacific University and San Francisco Theological Seminary. He was an interfaith chaplain and Presbyterian minister for many years. He has been a special education instructor in a private school and the director of a county emergency shelter. For six years he was the manager of two cooperative homes for independent seniors.

Chris has taught courses at Dominican University of California, Cherry Hill Seminary, College of Marin and Blue Ridge Community College. He currently teaches courses on Freethought at the Reuter Center on the campus of the University of North Carolina, Asheville. He writes the weekly "Highland Views" column for the Asheville Citizen-Times.

His numerous books include:
From Faith to Freethought
Simply Secular
Friendly Freethinker
Broken Bridges
A Freethinker's Gospel

Meditations of John Muir
My Address is a River

Chris is married to Carol Hovis, a Presbyterian minister and spiritual director. They live in the Blue Ridge Mountains in Asheville, North Carolina, where Nature is, day by day, enough.

For more information:
Friendly Freethinker (www.chighland.com)

To contact Chris:
chris.highland@gmail.com